SPEECHES, SERMONS, PICTURES, AND OFFICIAL DOCUMENTS

from

THE EPISCOPAL SYNOD OF AMERICA
Founded at Fort Worth, Texas, June 3, 1989

The Rt. Rev. A. Donald Davies,
General Editor

Speeches Transcribed by Carol Zager
and
Edited by David Peter Mills

Photos as indicated by Marjorie Manning Vaughn, THE CHRISTIAN CHALLENGE, Washington, D.C.

©1990 by The Episcopal Synod of America

All rights reserved. No part of this book may be reproduced, stored in a retrieval system, or transmitted, in any form or by any means, electronic, mechanical, photocopying, recording, or otherwise, without the written permission of the publisher.

Morehouse Publishing

Editorial Office
78 Danbury Road
Wilton, CT 06897

Corporate Office
P.O. Box 1321
Harrisburg, PA 17105

Library of Congress Cataloging-in-Publication Data

Episcopal Synod of America. Founding Meeting (1989: Fort Worth, Texas)
    The Episcopal Synod of America: a collection of historic documents from the Founding Meeting/general editor, A. Donald Davies: speeches edited by David Peter Mills.
    p. cm.
    Founding Meeting held June 1–3, 1989, Fort Worth, Texas
    ISBN 0-8192-1534-1
    1. Episcopal Synod of America—History—Sources. 2. Episcopal Church—Parties and movements—Congresses. 3. Anglican Communion—Parties and movements—Congresses. 4. Ordination of women—Anglican Communion—Congresses. I. Davies, A. Donald (Archibald Donald). II. Mills, David Peter. III. Title.
BX5820.E54   1989
283—dc20
                                                                          90-37478
                                                                          CIP

Printed in the United States of America
by
BSC Litho
Harrisburg, Pennsylvania

Contents

Introduction v
    The Right Reverend Clarence C. Pope, Jr.

Synod Speakers
Thursday, June 1, 1989 1
    Sermon at the Opening Eucharist
        The Reverend Andrew Craig Mead 3
    Opening Addresses
        The Right Reverend Clarence C. Pope, Jr. 13
        The Right Reverend Edward H. MacBurney 21
        The Right Reverend John-David Schofield 29

Friday, June 2, 1989 41
    Homily at Morning Prayer
        The Reverend Roger Beckwith 43
    The Voice of the Wider Communion
        The Right Reverend and Right Honorable Graham Leonard 53
        The Right Reverend Frederick C. Darwent 61
        The Right Reverend George M. Sessford 63
        The Right Reverend Harry S. Tevi 67
        Mr. Maurice Chandler, Esq., C.B.E. 69
        Mr. Oswald Clark, C.B.E. 71
        The Right Reverend John Hazlewood 75
    Address: The Beauty of Holiness in the Vineyard of God
        The Reverend Dr. William Ralston, Jr. 79
    Sermon at Evensong
        The Reverend Canon Christopher Colven 89

Saturday, June 3, 1989
    Homily at Morning Prayer
        The Reverend Roger Beckwith 95
    Sermon at the Closing Eucharist
        The Right Reverend Clarence C. Pope, Jr. 101

Appendices 105

The Rt. Reverend Clarence C. Pope, President of the Episcopal Synod of America.

Introduction

One of the most compelling things about Anglicanism is the claim to ancient roots deeply imbedded in the rich spiritual soil of apostolic times. The Church of England and the churches that derive from her are noted for holding steadfastly to that which was commonly held by all Christians at one time. Indeed, great emphasis is placed on the fact that Anglicans have no doctrines of their own, only those received from the ancient Catholic Church, grounded in Holy Scripture and the Tradition and filtered through the "Englishness" of our heritage.

This graceful and faithful approach to the practice of Christianity has had several challenges in the course of the history of Anglicanism, and it would seem that another testing time is now at hand. As in the past, when impending disaster gave way to a stronger church, so we must believe that such will be the case again. However, without a strong and faithful witness in this modern age of instant communication there is the real possibility that, at least in parts of the Anglican world, a radical departure from that which has always been believed will be inevitable. Faith and morals in their commonly held biblical and historical sense are being severely challenged, especially in the United States and Canada.

The addresses and sermons that follow were given in early June, 1989 at the founding of the Episcopal Synod of America, an organization that will give structure and voice to the many throughout Anglicanism who are concerned about the present crisis. This was an event of immense importance to the churches of the Anglican Communion and the presence and participation of prominent bishops, other clergy, and laymen from throughout the world is prime evidence for such a claim. June 1, 2, and 3, 1989, in Fort Worth, Texas, are days long to be remembered, and what you are about to read is reflective of their importance.

> The Right Reverend Clarence C. Pope, Jr.
> Bishop of Fort Worth
> President, Episcopal Synod of America

Synod Speakers
In order of speeches:

The Reverend Andrew Craig Mead, B.D. (Yale), B. Litt. (Keble College, Oxford)
Rector, Church of the Advent, Boston, MA
National Council of ECM, Society of the Holy Cross, Catholic Clerical Union

The Right Reverend Clarence C. Pope, Jr., M.Div. (The University of the South), D.D. (Nashotah House), D.D. (The University of the South)
Bishop of Fort Worth
Formerly Rector, St. Luke's, Baton Rouge
President, The Episcopal Synod of America
President, The Evangelical and Catholic Mission

The Right Reverend Edward H. MacBurney, M.Div. (Berkeley Divinity School), D.D. (Nashotah House)
Bishop of Quincy
Vice President, The Episcopal Synod of America
Vice President, The Evangelical and Catholic Mission
Board Member, St. Jude's Ranch for Children

The Right Reverend John-David Schofield, M.Div. (General Theological Seminary)
Bishop of San Joaquin
External Member, Byzantine Monastery of the Holy Transfiguration
Nationally known Retreat Leader and Spiritual Director
National Council, The Evangelical and Catholic Mission
Founding Member, Episcopal Charismatic Fellowship (now Episcopal Renewal Ministries)

The Reverend Dr. Roger Beckwith, M.A. (Oxon), M.S., B.D.
Warden, Latimer House, Oxford
Joint Secretary, The Association for The Apostolic Ministry
Most Recent Book: *The Old Testament Canon of the New Testament Church*

The Right Reverend and Right Honorable Graham Leonard
Bishop of London

The Right Reverend Frederick C. Darwent
Bishop of Aberdeen and Orkney, The Episcopal Church of Scotland

The Right Reverend George M. Sessford
Bishop of Moray Ross and Caithness, The Episcopal Church of Scotland

The Right Reverend Harry S. Tevi
Bishop of Vanuatu, The Province of Melanesia

Mr. Maurice Chandler
Member, General Synod of the Church of England
President, The Association for the Apostolic Ministry

Mr. Oswald Clark
Member of the Steering Committee of General Synod of the Church of England

The Right Reverend John Hazlewood
Bishop of Ballarat, The Anglican Church of Australia

The Reverend Dr. William Ralston, Jr., S.T.B., S.T.M., D.D.
Rector, St. John's, Savannah
Formerly Professor of Theology, University of the South

The Reverend Canon Christopher Colven
Master of the Society of the Holy Cross
Honorary Canon of Norwich Cathedral
Vicar of St. Stephen's, Gloucester Road, South Kensington
Formerly Administrator of the Shrine of Our Lady of Walsingham

Thursday, June 1, 1989

Sermon at the Opening Eucharist
The Reverend Andrew Craig Mead

Pilate said to him, "So you are a king?" Jesus answered, "You say that I am a king. For this I was born, and for this I have come into the world, to bear witness to the truth. Everyone who is of the truth hears my voice." (John 18:37, RSV)

Alleluia, Christ is risen! The Lord is risen indeed! Alleluia.

In the name of the living God: the Father, the Son, and the Holy Ghost.

My dearly beloved friends: Fathers-in-God, fellow priests and deacons, brothers and sisters in the family of Christ Jesus: the grace of our Lord Jesus Christ, the love of God, and the fellowship of the Holy Spirit be with us all.

I have been praying for this synod for months now—ever since it was called for—as I am sure you have been praying, that, putting away all anger and malice, all displeasure and trouble, all discord and uncharitableness, we will come together in the name of Jesus alone and be open to and guided by his Holy Spirit, to the glory of the Father. I have prayed that we will consequently be empowered by the Spirit of Holiness with courage, boldness, truthful speech, wisdom, good humor, and charity. May the Lord grant our prayers and pour upon us abundantly far more than we can even ask or imagine! AMEN.

A Disclaimer

I need to begin this sermon with a disclaimer. My current call and office in the church is as rector of the Church of the Advent, Boston, Massachusetts. I love that church and my calling as its rector, profoundly; I serve there with "grateful affection."

Many of you may know of the Advent's reputation as a venerable institution of the Anglo-Catholic movement in the Episcopal Church, having been incorporated in 1844, in the words of our constitution, "to bring to a portion of the City of Boston the ministrations of the Holy Catholic Church." By the grace of God and the intercession of many saints, she continues faithful to that charter.

But I need to add that I stand before you today, not so much as the rector of the Advent, but as Andrew Craig Mead, priest, period. This disclaimer is necessary for the truth's sake. First of all, you should know that, in spite of *and because of* its heritage, the Advent is a diverse congregation in every sense. We are a microcosm of the Episcopal Church, of the Anglo-Catholic movement, and indeed, in many ways, of the whole American Christian scene.

We have people, in the pews and in a few places of responsibility, who, for example, work hard for "gay rights" and even for the blessing of same-sex relationships. We have some who passionately favor women bishops; we have a leader who demonstrates against laboratory work leading to the development of nuclear weapons; we have political opinions of all sorts, including my own, which are, of course, excellent. We have a vestry member who sits on the very standing committee of the Diocese of Massachusetts that refused to give its consent to the consecration of my beloved friend Bishop Edward MacBurney simply because he has views on the ordination of women that are just like mine (perhaps a bit more moderate than mine!).

We also have many good souls who have signed the synod "Declaration," including some parish leaders who are with us at this synod, and we have a great many more at home who are praying fervently for us. These latter are not necessarily all at one with us in our position; but they are praying for me and us, and they *wish us well* in Christ Jesus. I think they represent all people of goodwill in the Church. They are our fellow members in the Body of Christ. We are here *for them, too,* whether they agree with us in everything or not.

A Priest of the Church

Now, why am I bringing all this up and making this disclaimer that I speak for myself? This brings me to my second point concerning the "truth's sake." I said I speak for myself, as a priest. That is, I speak as a priest of the One Holy Catholic and Apostolic Church of Jesus Christ. I was not ordained as a functionary of a sect or denomination but as priest in the Catholic Church. That is all I can do, speak as one priest, one individual, for the truth.

God made us, one by one, in his image. We come into his kingdom; we are made members of his Church, one by one. This is just as it should be! Jesus, in making his own good confession, did it before the church and the state, all by himself! We are no better! The servant is not above his Master. Let us follow our Good Shepherd-King: "I came to bear witness to the truth. Everyone who is of the truth hears my voice."

So let us begin by addressing our brothers and sisters who disagree with us. Since all life, including church life, is political, and since politics is most essentially local, let us begin as well by addressing our brothers and sisters at home who disagree with us.

I mentioned some at the Advent who take up positions with which I am in deep disagreement. I nevertheless try to do all in my power, within all that is good and honest, to respect these souls; and I most certainly pray for the grace to love each one of them with the affection of Jesus Christ unto salvation.

There is a little more that needs to be said on this score. It is possible, it is worthwhile, for Christians of differing opinions on subjects of lesser concern than the heart of the gospel to try to live in peace and charity together, to suffer through their differences, and to bear one another's pain and burdens. I trust that you are aware that I did not make these mandates of love; they come from the same Source who founded the apostolic ministry!

Respect and Love

We are speaking of respect within the Body of Christ, of respect for those whose opinions differ from what we are convinced is evangelical and catholic truth. Now, I have this to say to those who disagree with us, beginning with those at home. *I expect them and the Diocese of Massachusetts and the Episcopal Church to extend the same respect and love toward me and all those who are called "orthodox" or "traditionalists" in the Church. I have a conscience, too.*

I have a mind that thinks (I learned that I am what is called a "brain-dead Anglo-Catholic" by some so-called liberals who are obviously not liberals at all). I also have a heart that prays. I am a loyal churchman, too. I think we should take the Presiding Bishop at his word, when he declared at his consecration: "There are no outcasts in the Episcopal Church." *No* outcasts, not even biblical Christians and traditional Catholics!

Now what about that? My fellow outcasts, what is it that makes us tick? Well, first of all we are in good company if we are to be cast out for holding fast to our convictions. The man born blind was cast out of the synagogue for confessing that Jesus had given him his sight and that therefore Jesus must be quite a prophet, maybe even the Messiah. His excommunication led him to the Lord.

Jesus himself did not fare well with a church council called the Sanhedrin. He was a victim of judicial murder, ecclesiastical and secular. But being cast out, in and of itself, is nothing much except exclusion or expulsion. The reasons for the expulsion are what matter.

We began with Jesus; let us reaffirm that beginning. The conscience of the Christian is only properly formed if it is entirely submitted to Jesus Christ. Our propers for this eucharist are Jesus Christ the King, "Of the Reign of Christ."

His Kingdom is not of this world; it is far greater than that. It includes the rule of a person's heart, mind, and conscience. A Christian prays by the Holy Spirit through Christ to the Father; he thinks with the wisdom of God by following Christ the Word of God; he decides and believes and commits himself to the will of God as revealed by Christ the Son.

Jesus Christ's Revelation of God

We so-called orthodox or traditional church members are bearers of such names for good reason. We believe that the Church has received Jesus Christ's revelation of God as *God's Word,* that this divine self-disclosure is contained entirely and adequately in *God's Word written.* Not that the Church has stopped thinking (gone brain-dead) after the death of the last apostle, but quite the opposite.

The Church follows the apostolic commission: "I received from the Lord that which I now deliver to you." As Christ's Body and Bride, she draws forth from the Scriptures the essential content of saving doctrine, expressed in the creeds and councils of the undivided Church. As Jesus' faithful witness in every generation, she deepens her understanding of the mind of Christ and bears newborn souls into God's family.

And she fulfills and keeps this trust only by standing fast upon that true foundation, *keeping the substance of the faith whole and entire without addition or subtraction.* These essentials of the faith constitute the first principles and deep core of the Church's life; they are the things for which she exists.

It is not so much that the Church has a mission; it is much more true to say that the mission has a church! The "orthodox" or "traditional" church members are living reminders of the Church's stewardship of these mysteries.

Possession by a New Spirit

All subsidiary matters of the Church's life depend on and revolve around the essential gospel. When they are elevated to the status of first principles, in effect to a "new revelation" (which has been claimed in Massachusetts), then the Church puts herself in the grip of a counterfeit gospel that amounts to idolatry, or, in modern terms, ideology.

The Presiding Bishop has said in his recent pastoral letter that he wishes "to affirm" us here in Fort Worth. God bless him for that! But he has also said in the same letter that he *absolutely* upholds the principle of women's ordination to the priesthood and episcopate. But my friends, that particular principle cannot carry such weight!

It is not a *first* principle; it is not an established principle, and yet it is being made an *absolute* requirement of Episcopal Church membership! This is possession by a *new spirit,* which reduces the Episcopal Church to nothing more than a sect with a new revelation.

It is a spirit that provides the authorities with a sharp, schismatic knife with which to cut away and kill all orthodox resistance—a power each of us feels in many different ways. To name a few: exclusion, personal ridicule, dismissal, financial and otherwise forcible pressure and persecution, job discrimination, public humiliations, and so forth. Many of us are here, having heard our diocesan authorities rattle canonical and legal sabers at us when it has been quite unpastoral and unnecessary.

Let Us Tell It Out

So let us tell it out: this is dishonest, untrustworthy stewardship. This forfeits the trusteeship of the gospel. This substitutes ideology and a left line of political activity for true theology (which has no official ideology or political "line"). This manipulates the reins of power and secures the approval of the Establishment. "This" is the reigning new spirit in the Episcopal Church.

But such a spirit cannot be of God and his Christ; *it cannot be the Holy Spirit.* I think the new spirit is unclean. For why would the Spirit of God need to use coercion and intimidation, to guide his Church into all the truth? The holy orders of bishop and priest are important, but they are not the first principles of the faith. General Convention and synods are important, but they are not the sources of new revelations to bind the faithful.

We have attested to the authentic apostolic witness of the great ecumenical councils of the undivided Church. We have also seen that witness reaffirmed in the title deeds of classical Anglicanism. We have seen it in the biblical confessions of the Evangelical and Reformed Christians. We have most recently seen it in the great Second Vatican Council of the Roman Church and in the Petrine witness of the popes. And we have seen it in the heroic witness of the Eastern Orthodox churches.

So you can see we may be regarded as outcasts by the leaders of a dwindling American denomination. But we are in very good company, and we have a lot of it! So we should take courage by looking around at the Christian family and at the faithful witness of the saints of the Holy Catholic Church.

The Advent's First Rector

I began with a disclaimer of my office as the rector of the Church of the Advent. Let me begin my conclusion with a story about our first rector and our early days. Enshrined in our All Saints chapel reredos is a plain, flat, unadorned wood cross with some gold paint on it. That cross once was the principal cross in our first church building. The bishop of Massachusetts came to visit in 1845 and was not pleased with it, among other things, and with some angry agitation, demanded that the rector take it down.

This the rector politely but firmly declined to do. Subsequent parish history was not easy. The bishop wouldn't visit; extraordinary measures had to be taken by the rector to get his people confirmed —processions to other parish churches were an annual event for nearly a decade! But eventually (after the first rector's death and the election of an Anglo-Catholic missionary bishop as the second rector) it worked out, with the House of Bishops cooperating.

But do you know what? The wood cross and those other Catholic things that were objected to were still there! And they are to this very day. That was on account of a little quiet but firm courage by a few saints 150 years ago, in Boston no less!

Now it's our turn! But think: there are so many more of us now. Thousands, I think hundreds of thousands, more of us—in spiritual unity with the multitude that no man can number of Christian souls around the globe now and down through the ages of the Church. It is a mighty array. So we must be strong and of good courage.

But we need to remember that this taking courage, though we are in such a great encouraging company, is done how?—*one by one!* So now let me finish my conclusion by telling the story of how a great bishop, St. Basil of Caesarea, called "Basil the Great," took courage and witnessed to the truth when called upon to do so.

The Witness of St. Basil the Great

St. Basil is one of the so-called Cappadocian fathers (and mothers, I might add) of the Church. He was born into a Christian family. His grandfather had fled to the wilderness because of the persecution of Christians by the Roman emperor Diocletian. His grandmother was accounted a saint. His father was an estimable lawyer of some wealth and of high character; his mother was also worthy in person and character.

Basil received the best education that could be obtained then for a Christian youth, at Caesarea, at Constantinople, and at Athens (where he met Julian, afterward the apostate emperor, and the great St. Gregory of Nazianzus, another Cappodocian father). Basil's sister, Macrina, and his brother, Gregory of Nyssa (another Cappadocian father), and another brother, Peter, are all accounted saints in the ancient Orthodox churches.

Basil was ordained June 14, 364; we celebrate his feast day on that date. He was elected bishop of Caesarea, metropolitan of Cappadocia, in a hotly contested and narrowly won election between Arian heretics and Catholics. The *Lesser Feasts and Fasts* of the Episcopal Church says that Basil was

> relentless in his efforts to restore the faith and discipline of the clergy, and in defense of the Nicene faith. When the Emperor Valens (an Arian) sought to undercut Basil's power by dividing the See of Cappadocia, Basil forced his brother Gregory to become Bishop of Nyssa.

Does this not give you a strong sense of *deja vu?* It makes me think of the Diocese of Quincy; Caesarea, of the city of Peoria; Valens, of Berkeley Divinity School!

Be Strong and of Good Courage

Enough of that. We laugh, in order to clear our minds, strengthen our hearts and gird up our loins: be strong and of good courage, like Basil!

One day the Emperor Valens dispatched a legate to Caesarea to attempt to persuade its bishop, whose personal attractiveness, persuasiveness, and holiness was becoming a major nuisance to the Establishment, to adopt the new establishmentarian religion in place of Catholic orthodoxy. Basil proved inflexible (or should I say resolute and resilient!), and the legate lost his patience.

"Do you not know," said the frustrated officer, "that I am armed with power to make you wince?"

"What power is that?"

"I can order confiscation of goods, banishment, tortures, and death."

"Find out some more powerful menace," was Basil's reply. "As for confiscation — he who possesses nothing can lose nothing; all you can take from me is the wretched garment I wear and the few books that are my only wealth. All my treasure is within. (Perhaps there was no pension fund!) As for exile, the earth is the Lord's, and all people everywhere are my brothers and sisters; I shall be home wherever you send me. As for death, that would be a mercy; it would admit me to a life for which I have been preparing all my days, having died to the world quite some time ago."

The legate said he was not used to being spoken to in such a fashion. "Perhaps you have never fallen in before with a bishop" was the answer. The legate returned to the emperor, saying, "We are beaten; the man is beyond our threats." Perhaps some other approach was tried. In any case, Basil lives in the heart of the Catholic Church; Arianism, an old form of new heresies, in history's dustbin.

My wife Nancy is looking for a bumper sticker to paste on our refrigerator, which will say, "Remember Basil."

My Fellow Outcasts

My fellow outcasts, brothers and sisters of the biblical and orthodox faith of Jesus Christ, we have been this way many times before. Now it is our turn. Our turn to make the good confession, come what may.

But let us remember, we are confessing Christ and the essentials of saving doctrine. The Church exists for these. Let us not be afraid of threats and bullyings. I know it is hard. It is hard in Boston! But Catholic faith and evangelical witness has just as much history in Boston as revolution and heresy!

It is said that the clergy fear most losing their pensions and that the laity fear most losing their church buildings. Let us put away fear. There is no fear in love; perfect love casts out fear. We are standing on the promises of God; we are standing on the Word. We stand on the Catholic faith, on the everlasting gospel. We stand on the title deeds of our own Episcopal Church.

Here we stand, and we can do no other! What have we to fear? Fear God alone; and let the Holy Spirit give us a mouth and a wisdom in the hour of trial and witness. Let us, like our Lord Jesus Christ, make the good confession. Commend all to God, ourselves, one another, all that pertains to us, to him who is able to keep us without falling unto the day of his coming.

May he bless this holy convocation called in his name. And may he bless his whole Church, including the Anglican Communion and the Episcopal Church, beloved to us for his sake alone. And now let us ascribe to him, the Father, the Son, and the Holy Spirit, three Persons in One God, all might, majesty, dominion, and honor, this day and forever. AMEN.

Opening Address
The Right Reverend Clarence C. Pope, Jr.

I bid you welcome and greetings on behalf of the bishops of the Evangelical and Catholic Mission who have called us together to do the work of the Church, invoking the blessing of the Holy Trinity: Father, Son, and Holy Ghost. You have come from all parts of the United States and from nations all over the world. Your concern for the gospel of Jesus Christ and his Holy Church has brought you here, and we give thanks to God for your witness and great sacrifice.

With Prayer to Almighty God

With prayer to Almighty God for his guidance and protection, we will undertake a work that will have far-reaching consequences for the Church here in America as well as for the rest of the worldwide Anglican Communion. We seek nothing more and nothing less than to provide a way to maintain and propagate the gospel of Jesus Christ through the received tradition of the historic Church. We want to be able to live out our lives in this way and to be able to reach out in evangelistic fervor to others that they might be brought into the saving and loving embrace of our Lord and Savior, Jesus Christ.

Society, we believe, is hungry for this kind of Church and gospel—neither of which is subject to the shifting sands of this present age, an age that has taken a heavy toll of family life and done its best to undermine revealed religion. Underscoring the disenchantment of the American people with the secularization of the Church, *Time* magazine reported in its May 22d issue that heavy decline is underway in all of what it calls the "mainline" churches, including the Episcopal Church. Among the causes cited are social/political activity with a mask of spirituality and "mainline leaning for liberal politics and low-cal theology."

The Word *Synod*

We have deliberately used the word *synod* to describe our gathering because, while being a very graceful term in itself, it is charged with biblical imagery. *Synod (synhodos)* is, in our view, unmistakably connected with the unique description of Christianity found in the Acts of the Apostles. *Hodos*, the Way, a road, a journey, a way of life, and ultimately, the way of life found only in submission to that one holy life, Jesus Christ: "I am the way, and the truth, and the life; no one comes to the Father, but by me" (John 14:6, RSV).

We who have come together here to take positive and constructive action to preserve, protect, and propagate the faith of Jesus Christ as received through Holy Scripture and the unbroken tradition of the Church are not a complicated people. We are, I believe, substantially singleminded and single-hearted. We are passionately devoted to the belief that God revealed himself on his terms for our benefit and that this revelation remains as given, despite seemingly inexhaustible hermeneutics to the contrary.

If our view of the Bible and the tradition is condemned as being too static and out of touch with the world, then so be it. Being somewhat of a pragmatist, I know what works, and I must observe that being out of touch with the world in order to save the world has been an aspect of the Church's life that is terribly attractive to those in search of salvation and meaning for their lives.

They Teach and Defend the Faith

One of the things bishops are supposed to do is teach and defend the faith, and that is one of the purposes of this synod. There was a time when bishops of the Episcopal Church were taken seriously even by those who were not of this church. But I am afraid the antics of so many, beginning with Bishop Pike is his last years and moving onward to nameless ones in all parts of our Anglican world, have seriously devalued the coinage of the episcopate.

There has been too much exposure to those pathetic attempts to catch up with a rapidly deteriorating secular society in order to bless it and make it alright so that everyone can have a good feeling despite the wretched things done. The Reverend Richard Neuhaus reminds us that churches on this path are doomed: "Things like that don't play so well the second and twenty-second time around. What was shocking quickly becomes silly," he wrote recently. If the Church is perceived as a reflection of what's happening in society, then the ordinary citizen will find more attraction in the world and simply ignore it or, if already a member, will probably drop out . . . why settle for second best?

A Far More Substantial Response

The bishops of the Evangelical and Catholic Mission (ECM) have from the beginning of the progressive crisis in the Episcopal Church keep a high profile and acted in concerted ways to attempt to recall the Episcopal Church to her roots and rally the faithful to biblical truth and life within the historic tradition. We have been joined in this effort over the years by very loyal and self-sacrificing lay people, priests, and deacons through the work of ECM. We must also note that we have been aided by notable and prominent bishops, clergy, and lay people from the mother church and other parts of the Anglican Communion, some of whom you will have the honor of hearing later.

While the work and sacrifice of our mission has been enormous over the years, we must now face the reality that a far more substantial response must be made than in the past. Gone are the days when we plan an annual congress, sometimes called a "pep rally," and then rely on the ECM newsletter to do the remainder of the job in between such activities. We must take action in this synod to provide for the preservation and propagation of the gospel of Jesus Christ as historically received by the Church and all that that implies.

The secular press is primarily interested in the vexing symptoms of our problem—the ordination of women to the presbyterate and episcopate, problems related to practicing homosexuality, the dangerous and seemingly unstoppable influence of radical feminist theology, questions related to how we shall address God, the authority of the Bible, the nature of tradition, marital fidelity, and personal morality, as examples.

We must emphatically emphasize that the underlying problem from which these florid symptoms erupt is the loss of respect for the authority of Holy Scripture and the embracing of a worldview that ignores history. Under these circumstances both Scripture and tradition are treated as personal possessions to be tried on from time to time. If they fit the current fad of the age, then all well and good—but if not, then toss them aside for more exciting vesture.

The Early Fear Realized

The early fear of ECM that the ordinations of women to the presbyterate and episcopate were not the root problems but signs of a breakdown in authority with the resulting potential for substantial alteration to faith and order has been realized, sadly. We believe that both the authority of Holy Scripture and that of tradition have been so violated by the actions of General Convention that dissent is discounted when appeals are made to the Bible and claims of history.

We have but to examine the years following the 1976 decisions to go against the historic order of the Church to see the validity of the concern of ECM as touching the far-reaching problem of authority. Would there be a reliable source of authority when other issues arose out of the ferment of a society that seemed to be embracing every idea presented, however outrageous?

The Church, which for centuries engaged in slow and measured deliberations, no longer enjoys such leisure. Blessed as we are with modern communications and the near instant transmission of information, we must deal with new issues and challenges in very short order. The truth of this is all too evident. We are now not only faced with questions of holy order but with the lengthy list mentioned earlier.

There is growing evidence that strong sentiment exists throughout the Episcopal Church not to trust the Bible when its teaching conflicts with societal norms and interests. The severely weakened marriage canons of the Episcopal Church, which give rise to multiple marriages with priestly blessings upon each, is a prime example. We now see priests being divorced and remarried in the same way as the laity and with the blessing of bishops. In fact, there is no real marriage discipline in the Episcopal Church. That was one of the first things to go when virulent secularism began its relentless march through the sacred halls of the Church of America.

If the Bible is suspect and tradition is not to be taken seriously, then we are without any recognizable objective authority in the Church. Under these circumstances it is possible to do almost anything in the Church and claim that it is by the power of the Holy Spirit leading us into new things, however contrary to Holy Scripture.

The Last Effort

It is against this background that we meet in what may be the last effort on the part of those of us who want to walk the pathway we believe is most consistent with the givens of our faith. We want to walk the way—the *hodos* of Christ within the tradition handed down to us from generation to generation. We can trust it; we know what it is.

It is our intention to make our response within the constitutional and canonical provisions of the Episcopal Church. The model that will be presented during our meeting will reconstitute ECM into a more realistic ecclesial entity, with structure and form designed to accomplish our goals of propagation and defense of the faith once delivered.

Over the years, as the plight of those of us who seek to maintain faithfulness to Holy Scripture and the historic tradition of the Church has become more and more difficult, numerous solutions have been postulated. Most of you here are familiar with the various possibilities: stay and suffer; form a parallel jurisdiction; join one of the existing twenty-seven provinces of the Anglican Communion; or create an autonomous province of the Episcopal Church.

With the exception of staying, remaining quiet, and ultimately dying, nothing seems acceptable to the national Church. In fact, the Eames Commission report, and the subsequent response of the primates of the Anglican Communion, confirms this negative view, with the possible exception of some sort of undefined "Episcopal Visitors" provision tacked on.

The Eames Commission

The Eames Commission's philosophical concept of "reception" is one we find most difficult to accept. "Reception" is the commission's way of dealing with a new idea in the life of the Church. The Church is to receive the new idea and live with it, evaluate it, and either accept or reject it. In the meantime, we are to live with it patiently.

The truth of the matter is that we are not living with an amorphous idea or a heresy that a group might hold for a space, such as the Arians of blessed memory, but with a new idea that has been institutionalized and given flesh and bones. Many hundreds of women have undergone the rite of ordination to the priesthood and now one to the episcopate with the expectation of more to come in the near future. How is it possible to take the theory of reception seriously in the face of such institutionalization even though the process is said to carry with it the possibility of rejection?

The souls of the people of the Church are involved here, and we must raise alarm when it is admitted by an official commission of the Anglican Communion that this new ministry is "provisional," even though we have believed this to be the case from the beginning. I am afraid that the Eames Commission has succumbed to the American way of progressive revelation and has, as a result, contributed to the disunity of the Anglican Communion by trying to paper over cracks in its desperate attempt to preserve unity.

The implication of all this is that we who hold to the historic tradition of the Church will have a very short future. By the time the reception process has been worked out at some distant point in time, we will have few of our clergy left, no bishops with jurisdiction, and few, if any, lay people.

A Way of Walking Together

If we are to preserve the faith and heritage to which we are committed, we must provide a way of walking together. Let us firmly declare and commit ourselves to the Episcopal Church and to the provinces of the Anglican Communion that it is our will to be the Church within the Church. We will not accept proposals that would make us outcasts or a mere dissenting minority. We must have structural identity and focus for mission and strategy.

To this end it is our prayer that the Episcopal Synod of America will have its birth at this synod of the Evangelical and Catholic Mission. The proposed constitution, ordinances, and resolutions spell out the details of our postsynod life. This course of action must be viewed by the Episcopal Church as our serious commitment to have a future and to preserve the faith and tradition of the Church, which have been our heritage since the days of undivided Christendom.

In the spirit of the Eames Commission, which emphasized that bishops and dioceses of our communion should avoid pronouncing excommunication upon each other over the issue of the new episcopal ministry, we declare that it is our intention to undertake our way of walking within the Episcopal Church. There is no reason why our proposed Episcopal Synod of America should cancel or impair our communion either with the Episcopal Church or Canterbury.

Ours is a legitimate position within the Anglican Communion, and we deserve the right, with all due assistance from every appropriate source, to propagate it. The Episcopal Synod of America will be a fellowship of bishops, priests, deacons, and lay people who have the privilege and responsibility to organize its mission and minister to its own people, uninhibited. Unlike certain illegal actions within the Episcopal Church in the early seventies that were later regularized, what we propose is completely legal and within the confines of the Constitution and Canons of the Episcopal Church.

Our Love for the Episcopal Church

In undertaking our new mission, we express our love for the Episcopal Church and will strive for her unity with the strong desire to be partners in mission. This is a measured and carefully planned approach that has the real potential for meeting our needs without disturbing jurisdictional boundaries of any diocese or violating the constitution or canons of the Episcopal Church. We are, after all, free to associate with whom we please and so to organize if we desire.

It must be noted, however, that should the goals set forth through the emerging structure of this synod be thwarted by forces who might wish to see us disappear, we shall immediately reassess our position and then take whatever steps are necessary to ensure the succession of the historic episcopate and to carry out our mission as stated. That's important, too.

In all that we have done to bring us to this point we have been careful to consult with every appropriate jurisdictional authority within the Anglican Communion, from our own Presiding Bishop to the Archbishop of Canterbury, the Bishop of London, the Eames Commission, under the chairmanship of the Archbishop of Armagh, the Archbishop of Sydney, bishops of Scotland, and from the Pacific and southern Africa and from every other province of the communion.

In addition, we have had consultation with many members of the General Synod of the Church of England, both lay and clerical, as well as members of the theological faculties at home and abroad. Ecumenical talks have also been held to give us a broader perspective. We have, in fact, left no stone unturned.

Opening Address
The Right Reverend Edward H. MacBurney

The eleven disciples made their way to Galilee, to the mountain where Jesus had told them to meet him. When they saw him, they fell prostrate before him, though some were doubtful. Jesus then came up and spoke to them. He said: "Full authority in heaven and on earth has been committed to me. Go forth therefore and make all nations my disciples; baptize men everywhere in the name of the Father and the Son and the Holy Spirit, and teach them to observe all that I have commanded you. And be assured, I am with you always, to the end of time." (Matt. 28:16-20, NEB)

What We Believe

And teach them to observe all that I have commanded you. Bishop Pope has given us an overview of our synod. My task is to suggest as clearly and positively as possible, what we believe. Whereon we take our stand. You and I know full well how many in the church have seen us—and the synod—in negative terms. We have been categorized as anti-intellectual and fundamentalists, as rigid and infallibilists, as bad losers and schismatics. The reality is quite otherwise. I think it is high time to set the record straight!

Anglicanism, the form of Christianity to which you and I have entrusted ourselves, is in itself a wonderful gift from God, wherein we discover both the insights and truths of the classic Reformers, while holding to the catholic Scriptures, the catholic creeds, the catholic ministry, and the catholic sacraments. I am thoroughly committed to an Anglicanism that seeks to be faithful to the apostolic faith and life as contained in Scripture and as understood by the councils of the undivided

Church. For ours is a biblical faith, expressed sacramentally and liturgically.

My hope and prayer this evening for the synod is that whatever decisions we make, whatever actions we take, they may be understood by Anglicans everywhere as being rooted firmly, self-consciously, wholeheartedly within the great tradition we know as historic Anglicanism.

A God Who Reveals Himself

And teach them to observe all that I have commanded you. We believe in a God who reveals himself.

If our religion simply affirmed one path up the mountain toward an obscure God shrouded in the mist, no better though no worse than any other path, then it wouldn't matter much what happened to our church nor, indeed, whether we remained faithful, fell away, or chose instead to climb by another route and another religion. But we believe that our God chose to reveal himself: through the world he created; in his people, the Jews, with whom he covenanted; through patriarchs, prophets, and priests.

But most uniquely and in the fullness of time, in his Son Jesus. So that, as Father Whittemore of the Order of the Holy Cross used to tell his hearers in those old-fashioned preaching missions, if you had been present at the Lake of Galilee and been in on the secret, you could have said, That one is Thomas. And that one over there is John. But that one! That one is God himself!

Christianity will be interpreted anew by each generation. But that interpretation must be consistent with the givenness of the revelation. We cannot add to it nor subtract from it. Revelation is a gift of God.

Within that givenness is the Church. When the apostles burst out of their upper room on the day fire came down, they were part of a community they had not created, for it, too, was God's gift. And that gift of God, which we call the Bride and Body of Christ, was to be a living witness to the ends of the earth. A witness of God, as he has revealed himself, Father, Son, and Holy Spirit.

Since revelation is a gift, it is our obligation to receive it. To be thankful for it. To stand under it. And to affirm that no present "revelation" can deny what has been given in Scripture or the creeds, which explicate those Scriptures. And we would affirm also a givenness for the Church's ministry of bishops, priests, and deacons, as well as for the sacraments.

We have come very slowly to Fort Worth. But we have come, finally acknowledging the prophetic truth spoken by a Polish bishop in 1976, before he became John Paul II: We are now facing the final confrontation between the Church and the Antichurch, of the gospel versus the antigospel.

The Authority of Scripture

And teach them to observe all that I have commanded you. We believe in the authority of Scripture, for faith and morals and for the testing of doctrine.

Many today are rejecting most, if not all, of the Old Testament. The moral law, as reflected in the Ten Commandments, is regarded as outmoded. Virtually the only test remaining for some of our brethren is that text from Isaiah: "Behold, I am doing a new thing!" St. John's Gospel is dismissed as too late and too questionable to be taken seriously. Except, of course, for chapter 17. We are asked to sit very lightly to biblical passages that relate to heaven and hell. Sin itself is thought to be too negative for our age of affirmation.

And St. Paul . . . Well, St. Paul is a downright embarrassment because he is hopeless about women and probably a misogynist. And the Book of Revelation? Leave that to the religious fanatics and the crackpots who ring our doorbells and harass us at bus terminals. Scissors and paste have not left us much to be concerned with in the Scriptures. (You ought to be able to take the course in about three weeks in any seminary.)

And it is unfortunate indeed that Jesus did not have the advantages of a Sigmund Freud or a Charles Darwin. Not to mention the truths he might have garnered from a German theological faculty!

And yet. And yet both the 1979 and the 1928 Prayer Books continue to require of all candidates for ordination this assent: "I . . . solemnly declare that I do believe the Holy Scriptures of the Old and New Testaments to be the Word of God, and to contain all things necessary to salvation. . . ." A recent article entitled "Heaven" in *Newsweek* says this: While the pulpit may be full of agnostics, the pews are filled with believers.

Truth Is Not Relative

And teach them to observe all that I have commanded you. Because we believe that God's truth has been communicated through the Bible and through him who said, "I am the way, the truth and the life, no man cometh unto the Father but by me," we believe truth is not relative. It may appear at times in shades of grey. We may debate what is a particular truth within a given context or what may be the greater truth. But we stand with Martin Luther: "God's truth abideth still, His kingdom is for ever."

Allan Bloom, writing in his extraordinary and important book *The Closing of the American Mind,* says, "There is one thing a professor can be absolutely certain of: almost every student entering the university believes, or says he believes, that truth is relative." This is the climate in which the Church must witness to the truth of the gospel of Jesus Christ.

Situation ethics is a disaster for the Christian believer. Because, while it seeks to weigh many goods and to balance many truths, it fails to take account of man's Fall and, therefore, of our sin and self-centeredness. George Lindbeck, writing in his book *The Nature of Doctrine: Religion and Theology in a Post-Liberal Age,* says this:

> The viability of a unified world of the future may well depend on counteracting the acids of modernity. . . . It is at least an open question whether any religion will have the requisite toughness for this demanding task unless it at some point makes the claim that it is significantly true and unsurpassably true.

Many have attempted, in recent months, to add "experience" to reason, with that three-legged stool of classical Anglicanism: Scripture, tradition, and reason. Experience, however, engulfs reason. For it means only what is true for me. It is personalized, individualized relativism but portrayed now as divine good.

The Primary Foundation of Our Society

And teach them to observe all that I have commanded you. We believe in the moral teachings of the Bible. And it is out of that context that we uphold the family as the primary foundation of our society. We believe that God intends us to be chaste, both within and outside of marriage.

We are for the rights of the unborn and for the right of a woman to choose. But we believe that this choice needs to be made *before* the sexual act. Or, if afterward, then that it be responsible toward the new life that has begun. We take seriously the marriage vows, for better, for worse, till death us do part. The serial marriages of our people are serious enough. But the serial marriages of the clergy are nothing less than scandal.

An Apostolic Ministry

And teach them to observe all that I have commanded you. We believe that God has given us an apostolic ministry and that this gift is shared with the Orthodox, Roman Catholic, and Old Catholic churches. It is the historic ministry of bishops, priests, and deacons. When a candidate is ordained in our Anglican tradition, it is never as an Episcopal or Anglican deacon, priest, or bishop but as a "Deacon, Priest, or Bishop in the Church of God." It is thus a shared ministry. A common inheritance from the Church of the first centuries.

We do not believe that we can, as a small part of the Church, change the givenness of that ministry without the consent of the whole Church Catholic. What is even more appalling is our present action, wherein we have acted unilaterally, as one province of the Anglican Communion, insensitive to the beliefs or intentions of the rest of the communion.

And for the first time in four hundred years, our own ministry is now unacceptable to much of worldwide Anglicanism. We have entered what has been called a state of "impaired communion." Apparently, for the forseeable future, we shall have two streams of ministry, side by side, within the same Body. We believe this is tragic and cannot be what God intends.

The Beauty of Holiness

And teach them to observe all that I have commanded you. Finally, we believe in the beauty of holiness as we have known it for centuries in our worship using the *Book of Common Prayer.* For we believe that worship demands of us a sense of awe and wonder. As it carries us beyond ourselves into that realm of angels and archangels and all the company of heaven.

For many of us, the 1979 *Book of Common Prayer* provides the American Church with additional riches: holy days, proper prefaces, collects, and antiphons, to mention only a few. Some find worship in the contemporary idiom helpful and appropriate. But there are others, too, whose spiritual lives were formed and whose spirits were quickened within the context of Elizabethan prose and the Coverdale psalter.

Let me affirm right here that we believe Episcopalians ought to enjoy the freedom to use either the 1928 or the 1979 Prayer Books. Surely the Church of England has given us a model in her own permissive use of both the 1662 book and the *Alternative Service Book.*

But because we affirm the classical, credal definitions of God, we deplore the continued activity of the liturgical revisionists, who seek to provide the Church with what is called the "inclusive language liturgy." The present new liturgy, now being discussed and readied for use and being used in some parishes across this country, takes us along the path that will, at the end, provide the Episcopal Church with nothing short of a new religion. For worship of the trinity of "Mother, Lover, and Friend" is not the God revealed in Scripture.

Let us be very clear about this. When we worship the creation rather than the Creator; when we affirm the nurturing Mother as over against the Father who is King, Judge, and Lord; when we image a *Christa* instead of the Man of Sorrows; then we will have embraced not a heresy but a new religion.

The Hour Is Very Late

You and I are here at this synod in Fort Worth because the hour is late. Very late. It is, in reality, the bottom of the ninth. We are either to field a team or we will lose the game by forfeit. Many wondered, in the years after World War II, how it was that the Jews of Auschwitz and Buchenwald could be so tamely led into the gas chamber. History would have asked the same of us, had we not come to Fort Worth. For we also were being led to a Final Solution that would remove or bury our witness.

We have been the victims of a culture that is both sentimental and fatalistic. Herbert Schlossberg, in his extremely important book *Idols of Destruction,* writes precisely of this and of us:

> While humanist sentimentality says that whatever is felt to be right is right, historicist fate says that whatever is is right. Unable to bring the historical fact into the judgment of a transcendent principle, it can only defend the historical trend it judges to be dominant, while deprecating dissent as the voice of the past, destined for the trash can of history.

We are here because we are not easily going to be dismissed into the trash can of history!

God Is Still Lord

Full authority in heaven and on earth has been committed to me. Go forth therefore. . . . I am not discouraged. Right here in this Church and across this land there are thousands who have not bent the knee to Baal. I am not discouraged because I believe that God is still involved: both within history and as Lord of his Church.

I believe that there remain tremendous obstacles in our path and momentous battles to be fought: against the principalities and powers of secularism both within and without the Church. But I believe that you and I can, during the important hours of this synod that lie before us, make our affirmation. Not only to shout it aloud here in Fort Worth

but to make that affirmation echo throughout the Episcopal Church. For we who call ourselves orthodox or traditional Episcopalians are entirely positive:
- Because we stand under the authority of God's Word
- Because we know Jesus Christ as Lord and Savior
- Because we have experienced the power and love of God mediated through his sacraments
- Because we possess the apostolic ministry of bishops, priests, and deacons
- Because we are the inheritors of a priceless liturgy
- Because we are members of the One Holy Catholic and Apostolic Church

I began with Scripture, and I'd like to end with Scripture:

> Finally, then, find your strength in the Lord, in his mighty power. Put on all the armour which God provides, so that you may be able to stand firm against the devices of the devil. For our fight is not against human foes, but against cosmic powers, against the authorities and potentates of this dark world, against the superhuman forces of evil in the heavens. Therefore take up God's armour; then you will be able to stand your ground when things are at their worst, to complete every task and still to stand. Stand firm, I say. Fasten on the belt of truth; for coat of mail, put on integrity; let the shoes on your feet be the gospel of peace, to give you firm footing; and, with all these, take up the great shield of faith, with which you will be able to quench all the flaming arrows of the evil one. Take salvation for helmet; for sword, take that which the Spirit gives you—the words that come from God. Give yourselves wholly to prayer and entreaty; pray on every occasion in the power of the Spirit. To this end keep watch and persevere, always interceding for all God's people; and pray for me, that I may . . . [truly] make known his hidden purpose, for which I am an ambassador—in chains. Pray that I may speak of it boldly, as it is my duty to speak. (Eph. 6:10-20, NEB)

Last, I would ask you finally to join in a prayer written by Bishop Grafton of the Diocese of Fond du Lac almost a hundred years ago, and it is as apt today as it was then:

> O Lord, who has revealed the sins of those in high places in Thy Church, who through the subtlety of Satan have betrayed the purity of the Gospel truth, by subtraction or addition thereto, grant us grace to keep the faith once delivered, pure and undefiled. AMEN.

Opening Address
The Right Reverend John-David Schofield

When a family or an individual is in crisis and there is no ability or willingness to recognize the problem, in some circles at least, this failure would be called denial. Is it possible that we are in such a state at this present moment?

Disintegration and Crisis?

Despite the fact that one out of every three Episcopalians has left the church in recent decades, we are told by the Presiding Bishop in his most recent pastoral letter that he rejects the characterization of our church as in "disintegration" and "crisis." Further, we are informed that the majority of Episcopalians' voice was heard at General Convention 1976, while the fact remains that the bare 51 percent vote was so tenuous that the House of Bishops had to meet the following year and make special provisions for the 49 percent of the people who had genuine questions about remaining in the church.

Needless to say, with heavy hearts many felt conscience-bound to leave. And many who are present here in Fort Worth were among that number. Since that time, the very pressure that the bishops sought to avoid in spelling out in detail what was meant by the permissive legislation of 1976 has been brought to bear on individuals within parishes, seminarians threatened with dismissal or lack of placement upon ordination, or candidates being considered for the episcopate. This pressure has reached new levels of intolerance upon those individuals—standing in a tradition of nearly two thousand years and with the majority of other Anglican provinces throughout the world —who have been seen to question the wisdom of the majority of American Episcopalians.

It is a concern, too, that in this same pastoral letter (read in all parish churches this past weekend) the Presiding Bishop neither mentioned the major thrust of the Eames report describing our present state within Anglicanism as one of provisionality—clearly indicating that the jury is still out with regard to women's ordination—nor did he recall for the person-in-the-pew that the primates stated, equally clearly, that councils have been known to err in the past. The decision of General Convention is not infallible and may well prove to be wrong!

We have a problem, a serious problem. True, it is pastoral in nature, but its roots reveal a spiritual malady far more encompassing than women's ordination.

King David and a Toad

Travel with me this evening, if you will, to the Second Book of Samuel, the sixteenth chapter. We find King David toward the end of his life. At a time when all of his labors should be bearing fruit, when he should be able to look out over the united kingdom that he had fought so hard to bring into existence, instead there is a broken man, forced to flee from the capital, Jerusalem, and deprived of his throne by his own son, Absalom.

Accompanied by those who have remained faithful, David enters the town of Bahurim where he is confronted by a little toad of a man named Shimei. Beginning at verse 5, we read the following:

> As King David approached Bahurim, a man from the same clan as Saul's family came out from there. His name was Shimei, son of Gera, and he cursed as he came out. He pelted David and all the King's officials with stones, though all the troops and the special guard were on David's right and left. As he cursed, Shimei said, "Get out, get out, you man of blood, you scoundrel!" The Lord has repaid you for all the blood you shed in the household of Saul, in whose place you have reigned. The Lord has handed the kingdom over to your son Absalom. You have come to ruin because you are a man of blood!"

> Then Abishai son of Zeruiah said to the king, "Why should this dead dog curse my lord the king? Let me go over and cut off his head."

> But David responded,

> "My son who is of my own flesh, is trying to take my life. How much more, then, this Benjaminite! Leave him alone; let him curse; for the Lord has told him to. It may be that the Lord will see my distress and repay me with good for the cursing I am receiving today."

So David and his men continued along the road while Shimei was going along the hillside opposite him, cursing as he went and throwing stones at him and showering him with dirt. The king and all the people with him arrived at their destination . . . exhausted. And there he refreshed himself. (2 Sam. 16:5–14, NIV)

The picture is a vivid one and really requires no explanation at this point. There are, however, two outstanding details I would like to call to your attention.

What David Knows

First, please note that the natural reaction of Abishai is rejected by David. David is convinced that God is in this thing every bit as much as he has been in every other event in David's life. God has allowed this thing to happen, and David is convinced that "this is going to do me good!" What a faith! What a relationship with God!

Second, because of his faith, David knows something. What is it? Perhaps the words of a chorus popular some time ago best sum it up: David knew that what the world didn't give, the world can't take away!

David's reign, David's authority, David's crown and throne were all ordained by God! The Lord would accomplish his perfect will through them, and their strength and permanence could depend on nothing else but God. If there had been failure and sin and weakness as there was, both in David's life and in the affairs of the kingdom, then painful consequences had to follow.

David knew this. He was willing to take the buffeting, the cursing, the pelting of stones, and the removal, albeit temporary, from his throne and everything his heart held dear. To run from the consequences of his actions, to deny that anything was wrong was Saul's style, not his. This time of pain was all part of earlier disobedience. And if he had it coming to him, then so be it.

No, Abishai, don't run Shimei through with your sword! If this thing is going to be seen to end in God's glory, then we can't react or rebel. God's servants act in accordance with God's law, in God's way, with God's timing. There is no other way! Choose another course and you have chosen force and self and chaos.

David's Deep Lesson

You know the story as well as I. Absalom is killed. David is restored to his kingdom. The deep lesson, however, wasn't learned at this point in his life. That lesson came much earlier.

Pursued by Saul who was king, David had been branded as an outlaw. His crime? He had kept the commands of both his God and his king. During the middle of the night, the Lord put the king in David's power. Climbing down to the valley that separated the two of them and then up into the cave where Saul was sleeping, David trimmed a few inches from the king's garment.

In 1 Samuel, the twenty-fourth chapter, beginning at the eighth verse, we read the following:

> When Saul looked behind him, David bowed down and prostrated himself with his face to the ground. He said to Saul, "Why do you listen when men say, 'David is bent on harming you'? This day you have seen with your own eyes how the Lord delivered you into my hands in the cave. Some urged me to kill you, but I spared you; I said, 'I will not lift my hand against my master, because he is the Lord's anointed.' See, my father, look at this piece of your robe in my hand! I cut off the corner of your robe but did not kill you."

David continues:

> "Now understand and recognize that I am not guilty of wrongdoing or rebellion. I have not wronged you, but you are hunting me down to take my life. May the Lord judge between you and me. And may the Lord avenge the wrongs you have done to me, but my hand will not touch you. As the old saying goes, 'From evildoers come evil deeds,' so my hand will not touch you." (1 Sam. 24:8–13, NIV)

Later David laments that he had gone even so far as to touch the king's robes.

Valuable Lessons

We have valuable lessons to learn from this. Whether or not we agree with what is happening or with those in positions of authority, we have no right to touch the Lord's anointed! Even after the Spirit had been lifted from Saul, it was not David's position to unseat the king. The king doesn't stop being king when he has failed or disobeyed. Similarly, we need to come into that same confidence that was David's, namely that the Lord is in control no matter how it may appear otherwise!

The reality of who we are as the Body of Christ has never been left up to the Body, much less part of the Body or 51 percent of the Body! Spiritual realities are just that—they are givens. We cannot vote God's kingdom, God's Church, or who God is either into existence or out of existence. There are limits to the areas in which we can define ourselves and rightfully legislate. Depart from this, and at best we can only become a pale caricature of the real thing.

The flip side of this coin is, of course, the danger of holding onto something that is not of God and thereby making it an idol. We can avoid this if we take seriously what the Eames report and, subsequently, the primates' report ask of us. We need to recognize that we, as Anglicans, are in a state of provisionality.

Openness to the Holy Spirit

I find it reasonable to answer a fellow bishop, who asks why I cannot ordain a woman to the priesthood nor consider her as a candidate for the episcopate, by pointing to the serious question I have regarding the possibility that such is truly God's will. I do not say that it is an impossibility, but I have yet to see how much could be the case!

To this degree, it is possible for me to enter fully into the period of provisionality with those with whom I cannot agree. I make no claim of finality. I remain open to whatever God would show me. But how a bishop who ordains a woman to the priesthood or participates in the consecration of a woman to the episcopate can say he is equally open to the Holy Spirit is beyond me!

Should he have the smallest qualm of conscience, his actions—it seems to me—could only betray a lack of integrity. Far more serious than this, however, remains the uncertainty that must forever afterwards surround the sacramental actions of those so "ordained." I have a question, then, about how open, how provisional those who have committed themselves to this novel action within the Church can truly be!

A Model for a Turnabout

Beyond this, what disturbs many folks is the ability of the Episcopal Church even to admit there may have been a mistake. Playing "what if": Should England continue in the direction it now seems to be taking to turn away from women's ordination and if the twenty-two provinces of the twenty-seven who do not permit women to be ordained continue clearly in that stance, is there a model for a genuine "turnabout"? There is!

During the interregnum in English history, when bishops fled during the Commonwealth period and priests were—of necessity—ordained by other priests and not by bishops, such presbyterally ordained men were simply allowed to "die out" with the restoration of the monarchy and the episcopate. They just didn't ordain anyone that way again!

The same could hold true, equally well, at the end of our present state of provisionality. Not unlike our forefathers, we could look back on this period as the "anomaly," as it has been described both in the Eames report and by the primates meeting in Cyprus.

But, the likelihood of such a turn of events is minimal at best. One has only to meet with those in favor of ordaining women to discover how few are open to any discussion at all. Uniformly the stance has been rigid to the point of saying the matter is closed. The political, emotional, and educational investment has been enormous. And, from all appearances, there is no way that such a commitment is going to be allowed to go by default.

On the contrary, we have now come to a point where any suggestion against the ordination of women is viewed, immediately, as arising out of male chauvinism, bigotry, and an unwillingness to consider women as equals. The question, then, is not approached primarily as a theological one but is seen as one of sexist injustice. Those singled out for particularly harsh scorn are the women who voted in favor of Episcopal Visitors in last summer's General Convention. They have been called traitors to their own sex!

The Deeper Problem

Here, at last, we have a clue to the deeper problem facing the Episcopal Church. It is both a pastoral and a spiritual concern. Our roots are no longer deeply planted in Scripture and revelation. Quite to the contrary, we now find ourselves in the position of judging Scripture rather than the other way round. Today's world, today's disciplines appear to hold greater authority than the Bible itself.

One bishop has, in fact, called for a task force to ascertain whether or not such a primitive book filled with moral and ethical injunctions that are clearly out of step with present-day America can—in any way—claim the allegiance of Christians as we approach the twenty-first century. Proponents of inclusive language are already protesting that both the Old and New Testaments are patriarchal and, therefore, unacceptable!

One priest preparing to teach at the graduate level announced to me personally, just recently, that the triumphalism of the Church has been destructive. He, for one, is prepared to state unequivocally that he is opposed to all evangelism, especially with regard to the Jews, and that Jesus was not and is not the Messiah. His thinking, and that of the Presiding Bishop's Commission on Christian-Jewish Relations, last summer resulted in a vote against the uniqueness of Christ, thereby dismissing scriptural claims and the Apostles', Nicene, and Athanasian creeds.

Clearly, it will not be long before those who have already dismissed Scripture as authoritative will dismiss it as any kind of moral guide at all. In some quarters, this is already an accomplished fact.

We Have Forgotten What Ekklesia Means

Where is the problem? One young priest put it so well. He said, We have forgotten what *ekklesia* means. It doesn't mean only "the called together ones." It means those who have been *ek*, called out from the world. It means that our vocation is to be called deeper and deeper into the things of God! It means humbling ourselves before God and his Word. It means an attitude of openness to the Holy Spirit breathing upon the Word and challenging us in every area of our lives.

In 1945, C.S. Lewis foresaw what would happen. In an address to priests in the Church of England, he said,

> I insist that . . . bounding lines must exist, beyond which your doctrine will cease either to be Anglican or to be Christian, and I suggest also that the lines come a great deal sooner than many modern priests think. . . . And if you wish to go beyond them you must change your profession.

> This is your duty, not specially as Christians or as priests, but as honest men. . . . Men who have passed beyond these boundary lines . . . protest that they have come by their unorthodox opinions honestly [and] . . . come to feel like martyrs.

> We have not doubted that the unorthodox opinions were honestly held; what we complain of is your continuing your ministry after you have come to hold them.

"A man who makes his living as a paid agent of the Conservative Party," Lewis continued,

> may honestly change his views and honestly become a Communist. What we deny is that he can honestly continue to be a Conservative agent and to receive money from the one party while he supports the policy of another.

> We are to defend Christianity itself—the faith preached by the Apostles, attested by the Martyrs, . . . we are defending Christianity; not . . . "my religion."

The great difficulty is to get modern audiences to realize that you are preaching Christianity solely and simply because you happen to think it true... [not] because you like it or think it good for society....

"Our business," he concluded,

is to present that which is timeless (Truth, Christ) in the particular language of our own age. The bad preacher does exactly the opposite: he takes the ideas of our own age and tricks them out in the traditional language of Christianity." ("Christian Apologetics" in *God in the Dock*)

As stated before, then, it's not just a matter of women's ordination. The issue is so much deeper. If we choose, at this juncture, to turn our backs on Scripture and tradition, we will—as C.S. Lewis suggests— "cease either to be Anglican or to be Christian." This is a very real crisis!

Refreshment on the Way

It would appear that Absalom has begun to marshal his forces, and David has already passed through Bahurim. Could refreshment be on the way? I believe it is.

Already some bishops who have formerly stated they would not allow other bishops within their dioceses have now reversed their decisions. And we must be aware that the primates make things clear.

First, they insist that a real, workable program of Episcopal Visitation begin functioning in provinces where there has been division over the question of women in holy orders and that no penalties be applied to those who seek to invite a bishop from outside their diocese. For how can one be penalized for holding to one side of an unsettled question?

Second, their words seem to indicate that a separate province with overlapping jurisdictions would not be acceptable, pointing to resolutions of the Lambeth Conference dating back to 1897 consistently deploring parallel jurisdictions.

Third, the clarity with which the American Church was seen during the March 1989 interviews by the Eames Commission meeting in New York, along with other concerns raised (more than likely) by the primates themselves, has caused the Archbishop of Canterbury to continue the life of this commission on a more permanent basis. What this can say to us is the seriousness with which the wider Anglican Communion is viewing the condition of the American province and the measures the communion is prepared to insist upon so that persecution and penalties will not be applied to those who actively seek to follow out the guidelines for which the primates have called.

It is encumbent upon all orthodox bishops, equally, to take seriously the calls that will be made upon each of us, for it will take all the courage that any congregation or individual can muster to stand against the tidal wave of disapproval, innuendo, and exclusion that can be leveled against those who call for Episcopal Visitors. But call we must!

And the support that comes out of our association here with one another can be a further witness—not to bigotry, fundamentalism, or any such thing but to the Church that is almost unknown; a Church in which many of us have matured as Christians; a Church which is unafraid to proclaim biblical standards for our lives; a Church whose even-keeled life may well speak to those who cannot accept what is being said and done in the wider American province but who have, until now, been frightened away by rumors of precipitous action and schism. An Episcopal synod such as this one may also become a doorway through which many an Episcopalian discovers a way to return to the Sacraments and Church he has loved and found nowhere else.

The Church's Track Record

The track record of the Episcopal Church has not been a good one. As you have already heard, liberals have violated both constitution and canon law when it has served their purposes to do so. When the church and earlier Houses of Bishops lacked either the courage or will to bring disciplinary action against such individuals, the end result has been the rampant disorder and rebellion free to flourish in our midst.

Imagining that political power, votes, and might is equal to right, the liberal will turn to canon law and abuse those who do not agree with him. Those who have simply held to the faith and practice of the Episcopal Church until a scant thirteen years ago are now labeled schismatics, heretics, and sexists. It is difficult to do business with such folks, let alone find ourselves "in communion" with one another.

The word has indeed gone out from the primates that we are in an anomalous state of provisionality. Clearly, such a description is putting the best possible face on what some of us have gone through. How are we to respond? One well-known theologian from ages past can help us. Dealing with a totally different question, he suggested that Christians resort to the least amount of force to deal justly with any area of conflict.

Perhaps this is the route we are to travel. In the past we have done little or nothing. Evangelicals and Catholics alike have been heard to whimper—if they remained in the Church at all. One bishop seriously suggested to another, in my presence, that the traditionalist was called to remain in the Church and suffer!

The Church Is Still the Church

This meeting in Fort Worth, late as it is in coming, inaugurates action that we as believing Christians must take. As Evangelicals and Catholics, we are not free to dismiss the historic Church, either when it is acting contrary to the Scripture, tradition, and reason it has proclaimed heretofore or when it becomes politically expedient, ensnared by secular movements, or spiritually corrupt. For us, the Church, even when she has lost a vision of herself as the Bride of Christ and his own Body, is still the Church!

We must enter this period of provisionality whole-heartedly. Where there is violation of its tenets or where true openness is betrayed by persecution, inhibition, and exclusion from positions of responsibility and decision making, these must be trumpeted out in the very Church that claims to make "no outcasts." Where violations become violence, the synod will not and cannot stand by, wring hands, and helplessly complain! Another level of action will be called for and will be met.

Our presence here in Fort Worth, including all those we represent, says we will do whatever it takes to remain faithful to God on behalf of his Church. Right now, in Christ, we have begun. Where we will end and what we will need to do depends to such a large degree upon our freedom to grow, propagate, and make a way for those who want to return, to return.

Unlike the Liberals

Unlike the liberals who are prepared to thumb their noses at all who disagree and go it alone, despite the wider Anglican Communion (let alone our fellow Christians in orthodoxy or in Rome), we as Evangelicals and Catholics have a spiritual and pastoral responsibility before God even for the souls who would at this moment take their stand with Shimei and Absalom and shout, "Get out! Get out!"

Therefore, fears, suspicions, past hurts, genuine betrayals all play a part in forming the heart's attitude that each of us has with regard to the Church. For some of us, we come expecting a level of communion, love, and trust that our Lord Jesus himself couldn't find among his closest disciples. We come looking for bishops and leaders who will not fail, nor disappoint. There isn't one of us who can make the claim. One thing can open us to the maximum blessing God has for us, individually, and for his Church. It is realized and released through obedience to him.

Your Heart's Cry

If your heart's cry to the Lord has been to set behind you anything to do with what could so easily look like an apostate Church, to be free, and to face into the future only with fellow believers, these last words I quote from George MacDonald are for you. Their poetic form should not mislead us. The challenge they contain, difficult as it is, is nothing less than the pastoral and spiritual responsibility Christ sets before us.

> *I said: "Let me walk in the field."*
> *God said, "Nay, walk in the town."*
> *I said, "There are no flowers in the town."*
> *He said, "No flowers, but a crown."*
>
> *I said, "But the sky is black.*
> *There is nothing but noise and din."*
> *He answered: "Yet souls are sick.*
> *And souls in the dark undone."*
>
> *I said: "I shall miss the light,*
> *And friends will miss me, they say."*
> *He answered me: "Choose tonight,*
> *If I am to miss you, or they."*
>
> *I pleaded for time to be given.*
> *He said: "Is it hard to decide?*
> *It will not seem hard in Heaven*
> *To have followed the steps of your Guide."*
>
> *I cast one look at the fields,*
> *Then set my face to the town.*
> *He said: "My child, do you yield?*
> *Will you leave the flowers for the Crown?"*
>
> *Then into His hand went mine,*
> *And into my heart came He.*
> *And I walk in a light Divine,*
> *The path I had feared to see.*

Friday, June 2, 1989

Homily at Morning Prayer
The Reverend Dr. Roger Beckwith

LESSONS: 1 Kings 19; Acts 20:17–38.

TEXT: "For whatsoever things were written aforetime were written for our learning, that we through patience and comfort of the Scriptures might have hope" (Rom. 15:4, KJV).

Hope on earth, and above all hope in heaven: that is what we need to carry us through. And the Scriptures, Paul says, were written for that purpose.

A Striking Fact

It is a striking fact, when you come to think of it, that Elijah, perhaps the greatest of the nonliterary prophets, was a prophet of the Northern Kingdom of Israel and not of the Southern Kingdom of Judah. Elijah was a man of action rather than meditation, a speaker rather than a writer, a prophet to the men of his own day rather than to the men of the days to come; though, because his acts were recorded by others in Holy Scripture, they did, in fact, become an abiding example to the men of after days as well.

Yet, when you reflect further, it is not so surprising that a prophet with this kind of contemporary ministry was sent to the Northern Kingdom and not the southern. The worship of the true God was in such a parlous condition in the reign of Ahab and Jezebel when Elijah lived that, if the Lord did not intervene in the midst of contemporary events and confront the leaders of apostasy then and there, the true worship might be extinguished in the Northern Kingdom altogether. And so Elijah was sent.

And others were sent also. Besides his disciple Elisha, two of the literary prophets, Amos and Jonah, afterward belonged to the Northern

Kingdom, and two more, Hosea and Micah, directed their oracles to both Kingdoms in turn. In Elijah's own day, there had been at least a hundred prophets of the Lord in Israel, whom Jezebel had put to death, as appears from 1 Kings 18. It is only after that massacre that Elijah can say to Ahab, "I, even I only, am left a prophet of the Lord" (1 Kings 18:22, KJV).

Rival Shrines

The people of God had had a hard time in the Northern Kingdom from the very period of its foundation. You will remember that it came into being through the foolishness of King Rehoboam, Solomon's son, which provoked Jeroboam to revolt, supported by the ten northern tribes. I am sure the reaction of Jeroboam and the ten tribes to a foolish king is not difficult for Americans to understand.

However, since the Temple of the Lord, which Solomon had built, was in the Southern Kingdom, Jeroboam thought it necessary to set up rival shrines in his own kingdom, as in 1 Kings 12:26–33, KJV:

> And Jeroboam said in his heart, "Now shall the kingdom return to the house of David: if this people go up to do sacrifice in the house of the Lord at Jerusalem, then shall the heart of this people turn again unto their lord, even unto Rehoboam king of Judah; and they shall kill me, and return to Rehoboam king of Judah." Whereupon the king took counsel and made two calves of gold; and said unto them, "It is too much for you to go up to Jerusalem; behold thy gods, O Israel, which brought thee up out of the land of Egypt."
>
> And he set the one in Bethel and the other put he in Dan. And this thing became a sin; for the people went to worship before the one, even unto Dan. And he made an house of high places, and made priests from among all the people, which were not of the sons of Levi.

Jeroboam then ordained a feast on the fifteenth day of the eighth month,

> like unto the feast that is in Judah, and he went up unto the altar; so did he in Bethel, sacrificing unto the calves that he had made: and he placed in Bethel the priests of the high places which he had made. And he went up unto the altar which he had made in Bethel on the fifteenth day of the eighth month, even in the month which he had devised of his own heart; and he ordained a feast for the children of Israel, and went up unto the altar, to burn incense.

This wanton alteration of the revealed law of worship, setting up a different priesthood, a different autumn festival, and above all representing the God who had brought them up out of the land of Egypt by the forbidden and degrading use of images of golden calves, was quite unnecessary to his purpose and was undoubtedly a great offense to God. The constant refrain throughout the history of the kings of Israel is the reminder that they "departed not from the sins of Jeroboam the son of Nebat, wherewith he made Israel to sin," sometimes adding, "to with, the golden calves that were in Bethel and that were in Dan" (as in 2 Kings 10:29, KJV).

The Lord Did Not Cast Israel Off

One might think that the Lord would even at this early point have cast off Israel as no longer part of his people and would have confined his grace to the Southern Kingdom of Judah. After all, an idolatrous worship had been set up, it had been set up by authority (there was nothing unofficial about it), and it was having a wide following —Jeroboam did not just practice it himself, he led the *nation* astray.

And yet, until the very end of the history of the Northern Kingdom, until the final judgment upon it at the hand of the Assyrians, the Lord did not cast Israel off. In the account of the final judgment on the kingdom in 2 Kings 17, we are reminded of God's long patience and his constant merciful warnings: "Yet the Lord testified unto Israel . . . by the hand of every prophet, and of every seer, saying, Turn ye from your evil ways and keep my commandments and my statutes" (2 Kings 17:13, KJV).

The Lord continued to have his *worshipers* among them, who, since they could not worship at the official shrines, worshiped elsewhere. We know this from Elijah's complaint that, under Jezebel's leadership, the people had not only "slain God's prophets with the sword" but had "thrown down his altars" (1 Kings 19:10, KJV), that is, the *unofficial* altars that had had to be set up to allow the true worship of God to continue. One of these altars had been at Mount Carmel, and Elijah rebuilds it in his great conflict with the prophets of Baal: "He repaired the altar of the Lord that was broken down" (1 Kings 18:30, KJV).

Even in the reign of Ahab and Jezebel, or perhaps we should say, particularly in the reign of Ahab and Jezebel, God was still at work in the midst of Israel. In this reign the leaders of the nation went beyond anything perpetrated before and became quite openly worshipers of false gods (1 Kings 16:31–33, KJV): "as if it had been a light thing for him to walk in the sins of Jeroboam the son of Nebat, Ahab took to wife Jezebel, the daughter of Eth-baal King of the Zidonians, and went and served Baal and worshiped him. And he reared up an altar for Baal in the house of Baal, which he had built in Samaria. And Ahab made the Asherah."

What was the Asherah? It was a pornographic idol of female form (I forbear to draw comparisons). And, having set up these idols, Jezebel then began her murderous campaign against the true worshipers of Jehovah and attempted to wipe the true religion out.

God's People: A Very Mixed Body

This was the high point of the corruption of the People of God in Old Testament times and one of their darkest hours. If we might pause in the narrative for a moment, it is worth reflecting that God's people have always been a very mixed body and that the hope of a pure Church in this life is simply an *ideal* at which we must aim but in the knowledge that we will only accomplish our aim in heaven.

God is very long suffering; he does not quickly cast off his people or any of his people. We should show similar patience, knowing that in many things we *all* offend. In the thirty-nine *Articles of Religion* ("our confession," as that great High Church bishop Lancelot Andrewes called it), one of the things we confess is that "in the visible church the evil be ever mingled with the good, and sometimes the evil have chief authority" (Article 26). Think of Ahab, think of Caiaphas, think of the Borgia popes.

The chief point of the article, of course, is to say that evil ministers can *still* be means of grace, insofar as it is God's Word that they preach and God's sacraments that they minister and until such times as, by the due exercise of discipline, they are degraded from the ministry. But in the meantime almost any enormity is possible.

New Testament Warnings

St. Paul, in our second lesson, warns the Ephesian presbyter-bishops to take heed to themselves and to all the flock (Acts 20:28, KJV). "For I know this, that after my departing," he goes on, "shall grievous wolves enter in among you, not sparing the flock" (heresy has always been peripatetic, and since the eighteenth century, Germany has, of course, been a major exporter of it to other countries, like this one). "Also from your own selves," Paul goes on, "shall men arise, speaking perverse things, to draw away the disciples after them" (and you have had experience to this, too, in the USA—of error locally manufactured).

Elsewhere in the New Testament we are warned about those who will deny the Incarnation (1 John 2 and 4, and 2 John—"antichrists," St. John calls them); about those who will deny Christ's Second Coming (2 Peter 3); about those who will deny the resurrection of the body (1 Corinthians 15; 2 Timothy 2); and about those who will deny justification by grace through faith (Galatians 1—anathema, "accursed," is what Paul declares them to be). We are also warned about those who will preach sexual license (2 Peter 2; Revelation 2).

One thing we might not expect it to be necessary to be warned about (at least in a literal sense) is those who preach idolatry, and yet we are: "that woman Jezebel" as she is called in the letter to the church of Thyatira in Revelation 2, "whom we suffer to teach and to seduce my servants to commit fornication and to eat things sacrificed to idols" (Rev. 2:20, KJV). We have not yet seen an idol of the Buddha erected at Newark, though no doubt it is only a matter of time. But the same bishop who tells us that he worships the ascetic Buddhas is also a champion of the sexual license of Baal. Such is the degree of confusion and corruption that is now possible in the Anglican Church.

The Church and Heresy

And have we seen the Church exercising restraint upon such heresy, as Paul requires? The question answers itself. "Sometimes the evil have chief authority in the ministration of the word and sacraments," says our Article 26. Not having been restrained themselves, they are certainly not going to restrain others. If unchecked, this could even lead to that great falling away from the faith of Christ, which Paul foresees in 2 Thessalonians 2, and to the fulfillment of our Lord's awful warning: "When the Son of man cometh, shall he find faith on the earth?" (Luke 18:8, KJV). We dare to hope that he will, but the implication of his words seems to be, only just.

To return to Israel and to our narrative. The people of God had been driven to unofficial action to preserve the true worship, to the setting up of altar against altar. We who live in a divided Christendom should be the last to point the finger at the continuing churches, who have done something similar. And we have now reached the point where we have no choice but to take unofficial action ourselves.

But I said we were returning to Israel. We left the narrative at the point when Jezebel had begun her murderous campaign against the true worshipers of Jehovah and was attempting to wipe out the true religion.

God's Intervenes through Elijah

And now, when all seemed to be lost, God intervened through a prophet.

With dramatic suddenness, stepping like Melchizedek out of nowhere, "Elijah the Tishbite, who was of the sojournes of Gilead, said unto Ahab, 'As the Lord God of Israel liveth, before whom I stand, there shall not be dew nor rain these years, but according to my word' " (1 Kings 17:1, KJV). And so there followed that terrible and very sobering judgment of three and a half years' drought, all during which Elijah lived in concealment.

At the end of it, he appears again, as suddenly as on the first occasion. "And it came to pass, when Ahab saw Elijah, that Ahab said unto him, 'Is it thou, thou troubler of Israel?' " Wonderful, isn't it, how those who turn God's Church upside down always accuse any who stand in their way of being troublemakers? So Elijah is not without an answer to give:

And he answered, "I have not troubled Israel, but thou and thy father's house, in that ye have forsaken the commandments of the Lord, and thou hast followed the Baalim. Now therefore send, and gather to me all Israel unto Mount Carmel, and the prophets of Baal four-hundred and fifty, and the prophets of the Asherah four-hundred, which eat at Jezebel's table." (1 Kings 18:18–19, KJV)

And Ahab, despite his petulant words, is so chastened by the judgment of the drought (which is not quite over yet, remember) that he does precisely what Elijah says:

And Elijah came unto all the people and said, "How long halt ye between two opinions? If the Lord be God, follow him: but if Baal, then follow him." And the people answered him not a word. Then said Elijah unto the people, "I, even I only, remain a prophet of the Lord; but Baal's prophets are four-hundred and fifty men. Let them therefore give us two bullocks; and let them choose one bullock for themselves, and cut it in pieces, and lay it on wood, and put no fire under: and I will dress the other bullock, and lay it on wood, and put no fire under. And call ye on the name of your gods, and I will call on the name of the Lord: and the God that answereth by fire, let him be God." And all the people answered and said, "It is well spoken." (1 Kings 18:21–24, KJV)

And we all know what follows. The prophets of Baal offer their sacrifice and call on their god from morning to evening without the slightest result.

A Catholic Sacrifice

And then Elijah offers his sacrifice. It is a catholic sacrifice, notice. It is "at the time of the offering of the evening sacrifice" (18:29, 36). He could not offer it at Jerusalem, but he did the next best thing: he offered it at the time of the daily evening sacrifice that was being offered at Jerusalem in accordance with the Law of Moses. (Thus, the Law of Moses did not come after the prophets—the figment of someone's imagination—as the liberals like to tell us: it came before the prophets, whose mission was to recall God's people to his neglected Law.)

And Elijah builds a catholic altar on which to offer his sacrifice: I don't mean *Roman* Catholic; I mean catholic not sectarian. "And Elijah took twelve stones, according to the number of the tribes of the sons of Jacob" (18:31). Not ten stones for the ten northern tribes, nor yet two stones for the two southern tribes, but twelve stones for the whole People of God. This is how we should always act, as "mere Christians" (to use C.S. Lewis' phrase), and resist the temptation to act like a sect. And where is mere Christianity to be found? Lewis can tell us that, too: in the Holy Scriptures. But I must let Elijah offer his sacrifice!

He tells the Israelites to make it soaking wet, so that it is as incombustible as possible, and then he prays. "Then the fire of the Lord fell, and consumed the burnt-sacrifice, and the wood, and the stones, and the dust, and licked up the water that was in the trench. And when all the people saw it, they fell on their faces: and they said, The Lord, he is God; the Lord, he is God" (18:38–39).

And, seizing the moment of the people's faith, Elijah proceeds to purge the Church: "And Elijah said unto them, 'Take the prophets of Baal; let not one of them escape.' And they took them: and Elijah brought them down to the brook Kishon, and slew them there." This was in strict accordance with the Law of Moses. We read in Deuteronomy 13, "If there arise in the midst of thee a prophet . . . saying, Let us go after other gods . . . that prophet . . . shall be put to death."

The New Testament method of dealing with such people is slightly less drastic: it is excommunication. It is called "delivery to Satan" (1 Tim. 1:20)—out of the Church of Christ, back into the unbelieving world, the realm of Satan. And it has a remedial purpose: "that they may learn not to blaspheme." This is one of the differences between the old covenant and the new, which are important to note, because, when you have noted them, everything else in the Old Testament applies to us, too. As our text said, "Whatsoever things were written aforetime [that is, in the Old Testament] were written for *our* learning"—us Christians—we are the same People of God.

Jezebel's Reaction

You will have noticed that we have not yet reached the chapter that was read for our first lesson this morning. But it would be foolish for me to end the narrative with Elijah's triumph and not to notice Jezebel's reaction.

The chapter we read began with these words: "And Ahab told Jezebel all that Elijah had done, and withal how he had slain all the prophets with the sword. Then Jezebel sent a message unto Elijah, saying, 'So let the gods do to me, and more also, if I make not thy life as the life of one of them by tomorrow about this time' " (1 Kings 19:1–1, KJV). If we achieve anything at this synod, don't be surprised if there is a reaction; rather, be ready for it.

The psalmist says of the man who fears the Lord, "He shall not be afraid of evil tidings: his heart is fixed, trusting in the Lord" (Ps. 112:7, KJV). This detachment is what we should aim at; but it's so easy to be afraid at evil tidings, isn't it, if they take us off our guard? We think that God has lost control, or perhaps he does not care after all, when really he is testing our new-found faith in order to strengthen it.

Elijah, apparently, was for once taken off his guard: "And when he saw that, he arose, and went for his life, and came to Beer-sheba, which belongeth to Judah, and . . . went a day's journey into the wilderness, and came and sat down under a juniper tree: and he requested for himself that he might die." And then: "He lay down and slept"—it's a bit of a help when you're feeling depressed, isn't it? But you must not indulge it for too long. "And, behold, an angel touched him and said unto him, Arise and eat"—a little food can help, too. And then it happened again: "And he rose, and did eat and drink, and went in the strength of that meat forty days and forty nights unto Horeb the mount of God" (1 Kings 19:8, KJV).

It was a journey of several hundred miles, presumably on foot, through the wilderness, down into the Sinai Peninsula, right to Mount Sinai (also called Mount Horeb) itself. Why ever had God taken him there? Why? Because this was the mountain where God had made his covenant with Israel in the first place, where he had revealed his Ten Commandments in earthquake and fire. This was the place where it all began. And now it is going to begin all over again, though Elijah does not yet know it.

I, Even I Only, Am Left

When he reached Mount Horeb, "he came thither unto a cave, and lodged there," rather like Moses, when God put him in a cleft of the rock here and revealed his glory to him (Exod. 33–34) "And, behold, the word of the Lord came unto Elijah, and he said unto him, 'What doest thou here, Elijah?' And he said, 'I have been very jealous for the Lord, the God of hosts; for the children of Israel have forsaken thy covenant [thy covenant made in this place, he might have added], thrown down thine altars, and slain thy prophets with the sword: and I, even I only, am left; and they seek my life, to take it away.' "

"And God said, 'Go forth, and stand upon the mount before the Lord.' And, behold, the Lord passed by, and a great and strong wind rent the mountains, and brake in pieces the rocks before the Lord." This was a regular way God had of revealing himself, not only in the mighty rushing wind at Pentecost, which we remember so well, but also in the "whirlwind . . . out of the north, a great cloud, and a fire infolding itself" in the first vision of Ezekiel (Ezek. 1:4).

But, surprisingly, we read here that "the Lord was not in the wind. And after the wind an earthquake . . . and after the earthquake a fire." These are both explicitly recorded of God's previous revelation of himself at Sinai: "And Mount Sinai was altogether on a smoke, because the Lord descended upon it in fire: and the smoke thereof ascended as the smoke of a furnace, and the whole mount quaked greatly" (Exod. 19:18, KJV).

Nevertheless, this time "the Lord was not in the earthquake . . . the Lord was not in the fire. And after the fire a still small voice. And it was so, when Elijah heard it, that he wrapped his face in his mantle, and went out, and stood in the entering in of the cave. And, behold, there came a voice unto him, and said, 'What doest thou here, Elijah?' " The same question as before, and in answer Elijah repeats his complaint.

And the Lord said to Elijah: "Go, return on thy way to the wilderness of Damascus: and when thou comest, thou shalt anoint Hazael to be king over Syria: and Jehu the son of Nimshi shalt thou anoint to be king over Israel: and Elisha the son of Shaphat of Abel-meholah shalt thou anoint to be prophet in thy room. And it shall come to pass, that him that escapeth the sword of Hazael shall Jehu slay: and him that escapeth from the sword of Jehu shall Elisha slay." Thus the idolators of Israel are rooted out.

"Yet," the Lord continues, "I have left me seven thousand in Israel, all the knees which have not bowed unto Baal, and every mouth which hath not kissed him." What had Elijah said? "I, even I only, am left, and they seek my life to take it away." And what is God's reply? "Yet I have left me seven thousand in Israel, all the knees which have not bowed unto Baal, and every mouth which hath not kissed him." We are not very many, it is true, and God is speaking to us not in wind, earthquake, and fire but in a still small voice. But we must not despise the day of small things, for if our hidden support is in the ratio of 7,000 to 1, we are numerous indeed.

And even if it is not, "there is no restraint to the Lord to save by many or by few" (1 Sam. 14:6, KJV). It is not ultimately important how many people we have with us: the important thing is whether we have God with us. And "if God be for us," as St. Paul says in the closing verses of Romans 8,

> who can be against us? He that spared not his own Son, but delivered him up for us all, how shall he not with him also freely give us all things? Who shall lay anything to the charge of God's elect? It is God that justifieth. Who is he that condemneth? It is Christ that died, yea rather, that is risen again, who is even at the right hand of God, who also maketh intercession for us. Who shall separate us from the love of Christ? Shall tribulation, or distress, or persecution [note that], or famine, or nakedness, or peril, or sword? . . . Nay, in all these things we are more than conquerors through him that loved us. For I am persuaded, that neither death, nor life, nor angels, nor principalities, nor powers, nor things present, nor things to come, nor height, nor depth, nor any other creature, shall be able to separate us from the love of God, which is in Christ Jesus our Lord.

AMEN.

The Voice of the Wider Communion
The Right Reverend and Right Honorable Graham Leonard
Bishop of London
(Church of England)

My friends in Christ: I'm going to try and talk fairly slowly so that you won't have difficulty with my strange accent. But I must begin by expressing profound and deep gratitude to you for giving us from the wider Anglican Communion the privilege of joining with you on this historic occasion.

You have had the courtesy of inviting us here to be present and for some of us to participate in this great event. That enables us to express our support for the courageous action you are taking. For I believe the most significant paragraph in all the documents I've seen is on the end of Resolution A [see appendix 5] which says that you are going to go ahead, come what may. Your courtesy in inviting us here also gives us a share in your efforts, as you seek to be faithful in your very difficult situation. Now, unusually for me, I want to say just a few words about my own personal experience. And you will see later why I do so.

Personal Experience

This year I celebrate my twenty-fifth anniversary of consecration as a bishop. It was just about twenty-five years ago that we in the Anglican Communion began to face the onslaught of liberalism, or whatever you want to call it. Whether it was my consecration that caused that or whether it was coincidence or whether it was divine providence, it is not for me to say. But that is the fact. It was in the early sixties that we began to feel the effects of the efforts of those who sought to undermine our Anglican position.

Looking back at that time, rather to my surprise, I find that it was as long ago as that that I first began to speak, as I have constantly done since, about the realignment, the massive realignment, taking place throughout the world in all the churches—something I have described as likely to acquire the dimensions of a second Reformation—between those who seek to stand by the fact of the gospel as revealed and given and those who advocate that it should be modified to suit each successive generation.

During these twenty-five years, I have found myself, not of choice (I would have much preferred to have spent my time entirely in the pastoral and teaching work of a bishop, in the parishes, with the people), engaged in what has become a battle. In England we have, in those years, had to face the problems of the proposals of Anglican-Methodist unity, of covenanting, of the undermining of our teaching on marriage and marriage discipline, the problems of homosexuality, and the pressures of feminism.

And we have had to face those same problems in the Lambeth Conferences of 1968 and 1978 and 1988. What is very worrying is that underlying all these things we have had to face has been an attitude of mind that, I'm going to put it very bluntly indeed, is critical of God—of God's way with his world. For underlying these things has been the attitude, for example, that God actually made a great mistake in creating mankind as male and female and that it's up to us to obliterate the differences as far as we can. Underlying these things has also been the attitude that if God had been wiser and more foreseeing, he would have chosen *this* enlightened age in which to be incarnate and not a time nearly two thousand years ago. And I often wonder what some people make of the whole thrust of Scripture, that it was in the fullness of time, at the moment of God's choosing, that he chose to reveal himself to us, a fact that gives us something that is not negotiable.

Now, I do not pretend to have suffered as some of you have. But I do know what it is like to be the "odd man out," to be accused publicly of having had a nervous breakdown because of the views I had been advocating, to have been declared persona non grata in Canada and not permitted to function within the Church there because I would not endorse all the decisions of their General Synod, and as a result to take part in a perfectly respectable theological conference that perforce had to be arranged under the auspices of a university and not the Church. I know what it is to have had a resolution of the House of Bishops of the General Convention passed about me, when all I had done was to care for people who had been expelled and give them what help I could, and yet at the same time, to be facing incursions into my own diocese of those who broke not only the law of the Church but the law of the land by seeking to minister within it. I know what it is to be accused of being reactionary and divisive and to be labeled as a dissenter.

On that word, I just want to make two points. First of all, the word *dissenter*, as applied to us, can only be justified on the belief that truth is actually determined by a majority vote. And I send you back to the Thirty-nine Articles, not only about how councils may err, but on the fact that it is given to national churches only to alter those things that are not of divine ordinance. With regard to that word I would also say that it can only be used if you are adopting an emotivist attitude to morals, by which you believe that what you feel determines the way in which you should behave. But my other comment on that word *dissenter* is this: I find it very strange and ironical that, whereas in the USSR at the moment the word *dissenter* is out of fashion in these days of glasnost and perestroika, it is to the Church that we have to look to find people so labeled.

So I do understand and share your tribulations. And that is why I have made these personal remarks to begin with this morning.

The Importance of Fort Worth

In these years we have seen the politicizing of the Church and the replacement of eternal truths as necessary to salvation by fashionable stances. These are now what are required of us, apparently, if we are to be able to be saved, not to believe in the eternal truths of the gospel. And we have seen, as I would say, the abandonment of the gospel of judgment and grace. To that I shall return later. But when we have this situation, what happens is that, because of its origin, secular remedies are offered by the Church for the very ills that result from the abandonment of the gospel.

Now what happens here in Fort Worth is, I believe, of the utmost importance to the Anglican Communion. And the presence here of bishops from Papua New Guinea, Australia, Africa, the Caribbean, Scotland, and maybe other places as well reflects this fact. But the crunch has come here with you, and we look to you to take action at this moment. In saying that, I am not minimizing for one moment the number of those who share our stand and our beliefs and our concern throughout the world, whether they be bishops, priests, deacons, or lay people. They are far more numerous than we imagine. Fear not, for those that be with us are more than those that be with them!

But even if, within the Anglican Communion, we are in a minority —and, as I say, I am not sure of that at all—we must not lose heart. Already, I think it was Bishop MacBurney—I may be wrong—who referred to that great biblical concept of the remnant, the remnant who remained faithful within the chosen people. And it is not arrogance on our behalf but the expression of our response to the calling of God to say that we are called be the salt of the earth. And if the salt has lost its savor, wherewith shall it be salty?

That is why this moment is of such crucial importance. We have to witness within the Anglican Communion. I do not want to criticize those who in conscience have thought other steps were right for them, but I believe that for us we have to stay and to be the salt that gives the savor. And we must not think in other terms. And we must be prepared to face the cost. We have to find a way of staying within without compromise. Now I believe that the proposals being put before you at this synod in the resolutions do provide such a way. And they are a way by which we can take the initiative.

Perhaps I should just say this, that I have been reported in the papers in England as having been very critical of any provision for Episcopal Visitors. What I actually said was that I was critical of the provision for Episcopal Visitors in the Eames report, which I believe, as I've used the phrase, to be fatally flawed by two things: First, the separation of communion from truth; second the requirement that the ordinary has to be recognized and accepted seems to me to be quite extraordinary. The reason why the Eames Commission was set up was because there were those who could not do just that.

Communion and Truth

Let me go back for a moment to my first point about the separation of communion from truth. Look at church history, and you will find, as the Eames Commission reports, there is the recognition of our unity, our communion or *koinonia*—blessed word—given by baptism. But from the earliest days onward, the implementation of that fellowship given by God has always been inextricably bound up with the responsibility of witnessing to scriptural and apostolic truth.

On the second point about Eames, I just want to make a point I made more than once at the Lambeth Conference: that, on this notion of reception, the assessment of a doctrine by the Church as a whole is right and proper in cases of doctrine. But you cannot apply it in the case of sacramental actions, which either have happened or haven't. And you cannot live in the kind of provisional situation that is created when you do not know whether the sacraments can be trustworthy.

Now the implementation of these proposals can, I believe, lead not merely to a solution of your problem, at least in part to begin with, but to the creation of a network throughout the Anglican Communion of those who seek to remain faithful and to associate themselves with you. I will remain in communion with you come what may, provided you remain faithful, too. And I have said just that to the Archbishop of Canterbury. And I will remain in communion with him. But I see a network of those who within the state of what is now called "impaired communion within the Anglican Communion" are in full communion with each other, deliberately and consciously so, because they are committed, as I say, to the scriptural and apostolic gospel.

Let me just go back for a moment to the question of communion. As I say, I accept what Eames says about the communion given us by baptism, but it neglects two things. First, one role of a bishop is to enable people, the faithful, to come to the sacraments without presumption. "We do not presume to come to this Thy Table, O merciful Lord, trusting in our own righteousness." We come because the Church has been faithful in the power and promises of God. And it is the bishop's role to enable people to come in that way. And that is why the bishop has the responsibility that cannot be taken from him; it is part of his mission as a bishop and has nothing to do with his jurisdiction, not theologically. The bishop has the responsibility of saying who may minister to the people.

On the question of communion generally, I would simply say this: that the Church of England, and thereby the Anglican Communion, has always maintained its continuity with the Church of the New Testament, the Church of the early fathers, the Church of Augustine, the Church of Aquinas. And yet, yet it accepted a break in communion at the time of the Reformation for the sake of what it believed to be maintaining scriptural and apostolic truth. I find it very strange that the Anglican Communion, which, in terms of the Reformation, owes its being to that break, should be the same body saying, "You can remain in communion, whatever you believe."

Now, the resolutions you have here, the way you propose to act, will not necessarily match the situation everywhere in the Anglican Communion. That we must recognize. But what you propose to do will provide a model that can be used and adapted; it will point the way. I hope that the proposals will be endorsed enthusiastically and wholeheartedly.

The Gospel of Judgment and Grace

I return now to the question of the gospel itself, the gospel of judgment and grace. It was an Orthodox monk who once wrote, "There can be no word of grace if there be no word of judgment." And where is the judging to be done? If all that we do is to try to find reasons for endorsing what the world wants, we must not be afraid of exercising our mission of judgment. That must be based on the pattern of creation, the pattern of creation in which, when we behave in certain ways, when we do certain things, there are results. What we sow, that we shall reap.

And we must not pursue a pastoral policy, however compassionate it may sound, if, in fact, what we're trying to do is to let people sow what they want but reap something quite alien to the seed. Also, we base our judgment on the gospel, on the Word of God as spoken to us, and we dare not speak of the Word unless we are listening to it ourselves and standing under its judgment day by day. The Word brings life, not death.

Now, we have heard already eloquent terms of how we are to proclaim the gospel. But to what end shall we proclaim it at all? Not merely out of obedience. We are called to proclaim the gospel because the purpose of God is that every man and woman should enjoy fellowship with God, union with him, here and now, to be consummated in the world to come. And what we're actually concerned about and what moves us here—which should move us if it doesn't—is what we are proclaiming to enable people to live in the right relationship to God. For remember that in the last resort, when we come to die, as we shall all come to die, all that matters is our relationship to God. We shall have nothing else to take with us. Nothing. And we are called to bring to people, in Christ, that relationship to God in which alone we find our true purpose and destiny.

I just add to my personal testimony at this point. There was one moment in my life as a bishop when I was particularly under fire, and I found it very difficult. Suddenly, as in a flash, I saw that truth in a new way that spoke to the heart of my being: that in the last resort, nothing matters except my relationship to God. Seeing that gave me the strength and the courage and the will to continue.

Penitence and Faithfulness

Now, if we are going so to live, two things are necessary. The first is penitence. That should be a mark of all of us here: A penitence which does not condone our sins and find excuses for them, which rejects the fact that we live in what has been called an "alibi society." It recognizes the fact that sin matters, that if we behave in certain ways, we become certain kinds of people. And ultimately we can become the people who can live with nobody except ourselves, to be left entirely alone, which is hell. Our penitence springs from a recognition that our Lord himself has borne the cost of our forgiveness. There we see on the cross the ultimate effect of sin. There we see the glorious forgiveness God offers to us.

Second, besides penitence, we need faithfulness to continue to the end, come what may. Our Lord bore the cost on the cross, and he did so to the end. He was faithful unto death. So he rose again. And our Lord was so faithful because he knew the joy that was set before him. So, with the sweat of blood, he endured. And we must see the joy.

And so it is that bishops and priests, in particular, must ensure that our worship is not the worship of entertainment but the worship of adoration—in which we revere and we get glimpses of the joy and the glory, in which we forget ourselves because we are finding ourselves in God. We must ensure that within the Church there is the teaching and the exposition of the gospel, there is the expounding of the Word.

And the laity, too—they must not only be regular in their worship and in the sacraments, but they must be faithful and apt to learn. I make no apology for using that phrase. We must come to worship saying, not "What is in this for me?" but "What is God saying of himself? What is he calling me to be?" Only when we hear what God is saying to us and learn to bow down before him in loving adoration, to rise as free people in Christ, to go out in his name, will we be able to obey St. Paul's injunction: "For this cause, because of all that God is and has done for you and called you to be, this is the way you are going to live, this is the way you're going to behave."

And so, because we see the gospel, we are grasped by it, the majesty and immensity and glory of God's work for our redemption captures us, and there is called out of us love and courage and faithfulness and compassion and joy. And we shall also be enabled to make a good confession and—please God, one day—one day—we shall hear him say to us, "Well done, good and faithful servant. Enter into the joy of your Lord."

Bishops David Ball of Albany, John-David Schofield of San Joaquin, Clarence Pope of Fort Worth, Graham Leonard of London, and A. Donald Davies.

The Rev. William Ralston, Rector of St. John's, Savannah, Georgia.

The Rev. Andrew Mead, Rector of Church of the Advent, Boston, Massachusetts.

The Right Rev. A. Donald Davies Executive Director of the Synod, and former Bishop of Dallas and Fort Worth.

Mr. Robert Randolph, Esq., Chancellor of the Diocese of Fort Worth.

L to R—Bishop Charles T. Gaskell (Ret, Milwaukee), Bishop Robert H. Mize (Ret, DeMaraland, S. Africa), Bishop Paul Reeves (Ret, Georgia), Bishop Victor H. Rivera (Ret, San Joaquin), Bishop W.C.R. Sheridan (Ret, Northern Indiana), and Bishop Hal R. Gross (Ret, Oregon), share a moment before the closing processional.

L to R—The Rev. Marshall Vang, Rector, St. George's, Schenectady, NY, and a member of National Council (ECM); Canon Brien Koehler, Canon to the Ordinary, Fort Worth; Bishop Clarence C. Pope, Bishop of Fort Worth and President of ECM and ESA; Bishop William Stevens, Fond du Lac, and former president of ECM; and Bishop David Schofield, San Joaquin.

Mr. Oswald Clark, member of The Church of England's General Synod and former President of the House of Laity, addressing the faithful.

The Right Rev. Edward H. MacBurney, Quincy, and The Right Rev. David M. Schofield, San Joaquin.

The Rev. Titus Oates, All Saint's, Ashmont, Boston, Chairman of the Synod Nominating Committee.

The Right Rev. John Hazlewood, Diocese of Ballarat, Australia.

The Right Rev. Frederick C. Darwent, Diocese of Aberdeen and Orkney, The Scottish Episcopal Church.

The Right Rev. George Sessford, Diocese of Moray, Ross and Caithness, The Scottish Episcopal Church.

Mr. Maurice Chandler, Chairman of the Steering Committee of the Association for Apostolic Ministry, London.

The Rev. Roger Beckwith, Warden of Latimer House, Oxford, delivering a homily during Morning Prayer services.

Mr. Joseph L. Vacca, Deputy from St. Barnabas, Omaha, Nebraska.

The Rev. Frederick Buechner, Rector of All Saint's, Thomasville, Georgia.

The Right Rev. Clarence Haden, (Ret, Northern California) (R), and The Right Rev. Charles F. Boynton, (Ret, Puerto Rico, New York, Suff.) prepare to join the Synod opening processional.

Deputies pencil in changes to a resolution.

The Gospel reading during the Synod's opening Holy Communion service.

Bishop Leonard addressing the Fort Worth Synod.

L to R—*Bishop Harry S. Tevi, Vanuatu, Melanesia; Bishop Gerard Mpango, Western Tanganyika; Bishop Philip E. Elder, Windward Islands.*

The Voice of the Wider Communion
The Right Reverend Frederick C. Darwent
Diocese of Aberdeen and Orkney
(The Episcopal Church of Scotland)

Good morning, good friends. I am delighted and honored to be with you, and I bring you greetings from the northern part of the United Kingdom, which is, or course, Scotland. I bring you special greetings from my Diocese of Aberdeen and Orkney, which includes the Shetland Islands. And may I also bring you the warmest of wishes from a list of people—only two in the list—my colleague Bishop Derek Rawcliffe of the Diocese of Glasgow and Galloway and my colleague Bishop George Henderson from the Diocese of Argyll and the Isles. He says that his is the most beautiful diocese in the whole of the Anglican Communion! But he's wrong.

Two hundred and five years ago, my friends, in my see city of Aberdeen, just on a spot quite near to my cathedral, there occurred a very special event: the consecration of an American priest, an American male priest, by the name of Samuel Seabury. He was consecrated by three northern Scottish bishops at the time. There were only four of them in action at that particular time; it was a very hard time for our particular little church in the northern part of Britain. The consecrators were Robert (Kilgower) of Aberdeen; John Skinner, coadjutor of Aberdeen; and Arthur (Petrie) of the neighboring Diocese of Moray and Ross. I haven't time to tell you anymore about that now, but I'm proud to say that in Bishop George Sessford and myself, you have the two bishops who stand in direct line of those three consecrators of your first American bishop.

The Gift of the Historic Episcopate
So, from Aberdeen, those two hundred and five years ago, came to you in America our gift of the bestowing of the historic episcopate. And we

can go further, and I'll stand up against anybody who gainsays it, that date, November 14, 1784, was the very moment when the Anglican Communion as we know it was born. And for this and many other reasons, I am proud to be an Episcopalian of the Scottish variety, and I value greatly my membership in the Anglican Communion. I am sure all of you do, too, and we mustn't lose it!

I don't know about you, but I am sure that Seabury would have been turning in his grave at some of the events of the last two decades in this great church of yours. We probably all know the story of Rotating Jones. Who knows? In the heavenly realm, Seabury may be known as Swirling Sam! But I am absolutely certain that he would be applauding this synod and all its aims and all its objectives. And in Seabury's name, in the name of the first bishop in America, God bless you in all you are doing.

The Voice of the Wider Communion
The Right Reverend George M. Sessford
Bishop of Moray, Ross, and Caithness
(The Episcopal Church of Scotland)

The Seabury Saga

Bishops, fathers, and brethren: it's an enormous privilege to be here with you. I want to share just one brief thought about the Seabury saga. I don't know whether it's generally known or not, but, in exchange for us giving you Seabury as a bishop, you in America agreed to have the Scottish liturgy as the basis of your liturgical tradition. And that, if you like, was a form of concordat. I wish now—how I wish, with the gift of hindsight—that the concordat had agreed somehow or other, to include a phrase regarding the preservation inviolate of the apostolic ministry, too!

Greatly daring, as I speak for another part of the Anglican Communion, I've been asked to say some words to you about your vocation and your contribution to the rest of the Anglican world. What follows may be a little controversial, and I'm sorry it's so. But there are others of us who feel equally beleaguered, as you do, in our situations. So I want to ask some things of you.

First of all, your Presiding Bishop, a few years before the Lambeth Conference, came and spoke to the United Kingdom diocesan bishops in London, and he opined that the American church was leading the whole Anglican world on the issue of what he called "new understandings of ministry." I dare to suggest that those undaunted leadership qualities that came from America had one fatal flaw: the leadership was in the wrong direction!

But what I couldn't and wouldn't gainsay was that the influence of the American Church was and is absolutely enormous in the smaller countries. So my first plea to you, my dear friends, beloved brethren of ECM, is this: please do not, through a false humility and modesty, confine your witness just to the American Church. The rest of the Anglican Communion needs it, too. I challenge you, I beg you, to extend your enthusiasm and your insights and experience and certainly your great dynamism and put these things at the service of the whole Anglican Communion.

Repaying a Debt to the Communion

As a Scot who's always "on the make," I would suggest that you repay the debt to Scotland and to the born Anglican Communion of our giving you Seabury. Give us the sort of leadership that beloved Bishop Clarence and the others, the others, the colleagues of ECM, are giving to you, and give that to the world Church, too. We would be enormously grateful and greatly enriched.

As the Bishop of London has pointed out so clearly, it's not an easy vocation. Ask what the bishops of Papua New Guinea think, or others who've been slandered because of the lead they're trying to give. That leadership will be costly to individuals and to you as a group, but who said Christian witness was ever easy? And the Anglican Communion needs the new direction of enthusiastic orthodoxy, which I find particularly strong here and which you are in a uniquely favored position to give. ECM of America, your synod must move out from a position of beleaguered isolation to one of influential leadership and give us a worldwide Anglican movement of fresh renewed orthodoxy.

Please, now, ecumenically, help us again. In September, 1989, a crucial meeting is to take place in Rome between the Archbishop of Canterbury and his holiness, the Pope. I hope it might be possible for this synod to send at least two messages, formally, and I dare to hope, unanimously. One to the Archbishop himself, assuring him, as we've heard so many times, of our loyalty as Anglicans and our deep concern for the future of the Anglican Communion. We are not schismatics, but we are those who abhor schism and, at the same time, abhor heresy. And I think we want to say this to him. And we want to send a message to him assuring him of our good wishes and prayers for the future success of ARCIC, the Anglican-Roman Catholic International Commission, but greatly daring, could we possibly send a message to the Holy Father himself?

Catholic Unity

And I ask, could we assure him that we, too, and many Anglicans throughout the world, are totally committed to a cause of Catholic unity and to all that ARCIC stands for? We, too, share *his* belief, no matter what he might hear from others about the nature of the apostolic ministry of bishops and priests and the inadmissability of the theory that one part of the Church alone has the authority to alter and change the tradition of the whole Church over two thousand years. I simply want him to know that not all Anglicans travel the way of Boston to Rome.

The third point, the hardest of all to make, is perhaps not the least important. And that's the image and the content of the leadership that we ask of you and we want to share with you in the Anglican world. When I told two friends in Scotland about my coming to this synod, I had these comments: by a Roman Catholic, "Oh, you're a sort of Lefebvrist movement, I suppose"; and by a Scot who at one time had an advent in Boston, "Ah, mindless fundamentalism!" Now, I think there's a language difficulty here. The word *mindless* in Scotland means what you refer to as "brain-dead" in America. Two countries divided by a common language!

Please give the light of these jibes. *We* know that they're not true, but demonstrate that they're not. And I suggest there are certain ways in which we can do it.

Scholarship, Youth, and Unity

First of all, we can demonstrate that we are not "brain-dead" by the quality of the scholarship our movements generate and sustain. We do need a fresh, persuasive, lively, modern presentation of orthodox theology, the sort you get from the Bishop of London, if I may say so. And our movement must sponsor this: We worship God with our minds, as well as our hearts and our wills.

And second, please let us be a movement with an appeal to youth. One of the most encouraging things for a visitor to this synod from what is called the "old country" is the vision of so many younger faces among, not just the laity, but the clergy and religious, too. Younger fathers and fathers-to-be and all the rest of you: please, we "oldies" need your pressure to present, not what critics have called "British Museum religion," but lively, modern, adoring worship and scholarship that combines faithfulness to the tradition with sensitivity to the cultural context of the mission field in which God has set us. So often meetings like this in Scotland (I don't speak about England) are, as it were, "geriatric" in composition. Let our movement give encouragement to young people on the move in the Church.

Two down, one to go. The third and last point is this: just before I left the United Kingdom, Clifford Longley wrote an article in the

Times, and he pointed out that it takes two sides to produce disunity or schism. He was heartened, he said in his article, by the constant reaffirmations of orthodox Anglicans that they were not bent on forming a breakaway church. I hope our synod, if it sends a message to Canterbury, includes this statement: We do not intend to go away. We shall remain in communion with Canterbury; any breech or schism will not be on our side or of our making.

Fathers and brethren, I rest my case. The Anglican Communion needs you. Please don't forget us.

The Voice of the Wider Communion
The Right Reverend Harry S. Tevi
Bishop of Vanuatu
(Province of Melanesia)

Bishops and all the People of God in the Church of God: I am Bishop Harry Tevi from the province of the Church of Melanesia, of the Diocese of Vanuatu, near Australia. Out in the sea, there is where my diocese is. I bring to you, bishops and people of the Evangelical and Catholic Mission, greetings and prayers from the Diocese of Vanuatu and the assurance from the Roman Catholic bishop of Port Vila of his prayers for us, for you, and especially for the Church today at Fort Worth.

I was born a Christian in 1930. My father was a Christian way back in the 1920s, and my mother was a Christian. I have been brought up in the Anglican Catholic Church in Melanesia most of my life.

The Anglican Catholic Faith

The wishes of the people of the Diocese of Vanuatu are to remain faithful in that Anglican Catholic faith we have received from our fathers—the missionaries who came from England, like Bishop George Augustus Selwyn, Bishop John Coleridge Patteson, and the others that followed from New Zealand and Australia, who were faithful fathers of the Church of Melanesia. The Diocese of Vanuatu and the people of that diocese heard and experienced a lot of dominations in the war that at one time dominated our islands in 1942 and again by trying to dump the bad bomb in the South Pacific. And now in the Church, with the ordination of women and, more to say, the consecration of women as bishops, this little diocese with its Catholic doctrines that we have received from the Church of England—and we believe to be that very Church ourselves—do not know where to go. We have been dominated by outsiders, and now all this has been introduced, and this little diocese does not know where to go.

But when we find that there are people and bishops standing up with their people, the People of God, in the Evangelical and Catholic Mission, we have faith and trust that the resolutions you will pass will lead us all into standing firm in that one holy catholic faith. To add to that, my brothers and sisters in Christ, of course, as the Scripture says, the Lord is with us. I, myself, have seen his revelation. He has come to reveal himself, as those that we do not see are many, and they are with us.

I would like to say that if you find difficulties in areas of mission, there are places of mission open to you, even in the South Pacific. My brothers and sisters, and my brother bishops, thank you all very much for your support and prayers. The Diocese of Vanuatu and the Church of Melanesia will always be faithful in looking toward the guidance of the Holy Spirit, which begins to break out in true faith today. And I believe that you will lead us to go forward in the catholic faith and mission. Thank you all, and God bless you.

The Voice of the Wider Communion
Mr. Maurice Chandler, Esq., C.B.E.
Chairman, Association for Apostolic Ministry
Member, General Synod of
the Church of England

My Lord Bishop: First of all, I should like to associate myself with everything that the Bishop of London has said and, in particular, with his expression of our appreciation of the very warm welcome that you have given to those of us who have come over from England. It's indeed an honor and a privilege to be with you on this important and auspicious occasion.

But I'm here, not to make a speech, but to bring you a greeting, a message of good wishes [see appendix 9]. This message is signed by one hundred thirty-five members of the General Synod, six of whom are present in this hall. And those one hundred and thirty-five members comprise just about 25 percent of its membership. Among them are the nine members of the standing committee; that is more than a quarter of its membership. So we do represent a significant voice of opinion in the Church of England.

You, my Lord Bishop, referred to the Association for the Apostolic Ministry. Actually, the Archbishop of Sydney and the Bishop of London are the joint chairmen; I am the chairman of the steering committee. One of the things the steering committee has done is to help organize the greeting, a message of support, which I bring to you.

General Synod's Message

But without further ado, I will read the message, and then I will give you the list of signatures. The message is addressed to the convening bishops of the ECM special synod:

> We welcome the initiative taken by the ECM to convene a Special Synod of Bishops, Clergy, and Laity of ECUSA.

We share your concern at the continual erosion of the authority of Scripture and of the doctrinal and moral standards which are founded on it.

We recognize that current developments in ECUSA necessitate the provision of alternative orthodox episcopal oversight, and appreciate the careful efforts you are making to this end.

We assure you of our prayers and support both during your current synod and in the future.

That message is signed by nine members of the House of Bishops of the General Synod; by sixty-five members of the House of Clergy, including among their number both the prolocutors, two deans and provosts, eight archdeacons, seven canons-residentiary of cathedrals, and twenty-three other canons; and by sixty-one members of the House of Laity, including three members of Parliament and two of the Church Estates Commissioners.

[Mr. Chandler then read the names of the signatories.]

There is a second and similar message, but you can have too much of a good thing—at least I hope it's a good thing! And so, I will not read the message again, but I will read the names of the signators, which include nineteen bishops, three distinguished clergy, and one distinguished layman.

My Lord Bishop, may I ask you to convey this message to your president and your colleagues and your members as a souvenir of the message I have just delivered. Thank you very much.

The Voice of the Wider Communion
Mr. Oswald Clark, C.B.E.
Member of the Steering Committee of the General Synod of the Church of England

My Lord Chairman, Right Reverend, Very Reverend, Venerable, and Reverend Fathers, Reverend and Sisters, beloved all in Christ: We meet at a time of division, distress, and danger, and there's nothing new in that! At Cypress last month, the Archbishop of Canterbury reminded the Anglican primates that the early Church was not afraid of disagreements and rows, and certainly the Church of England has always been in danger!

Each century has brought its threat. A hundred and fifty years ago when the Church's authority and position as a divine society were under threat, an Oxford priest, John Henry Newman, pioneered a series of articles—Tracts for the Times. In the very first of them, he boldly put the fundamental question, "Upon what ground do you stand, O Presbyter of the Church of England?" But none of those threats ever justified despair and disillusionment, though each produced difficult days and sometimes decades of difficult days and years. And the growing Anglican Communion came to feel its full share of them.

Part of the One Holy Catholic and Apostolic Church

Yet, in spite of all, Anglicans have made no unilateral alteration to the canon of Scripture, no unilateral revision of the creeds. They have not tampered with the God-given sacraments, and not till recently have they sought to vary radically that historic ministry of the Church. And why? Not just to hold together the Anglican Communion, which seems to have been the prime aim—and nominal achievement—of the last Lambeth Conference. No! Primarily to preserve our claim to be inalienably several parts of the One Holy Catholic and Apostolic Church and, as a corollary, to accept that our authority as individual churches is thereby restrained by the obligations of our membership of the greater and higher body.

It was primarily as a priest of that One Church that Father Mead preached to us yesterday. It is primarily as a layman baptized into that One Church with all of you that I am privileged to speak to you now. And maybe it's time that the laity got a word in at this synod! We are not just financial or statistical units, and our role is not to give a holy, passive, "me, too!" Of course, I am a Church of England man, as you are Episcopalians of ECUSA, and like you, I love my Church, and I have no intention of departing from her.

Though of one Anglican family, we each have particular ways of expressing our common faith and order, and we value that ecclesial independence as particular churches. But provincial autonomy is not to be exalted as a principle of the gospel in such a way that each part of the One Holy Catholic Church is able to claim for itself the fullness of catholicity and authority and so feels free to do as it will with any part of the faith and order of the One Church and to abandon that properly restrained Catholicism that has marked Anglican churches from Richard Hooker to Michael Ramsey.

Sectarian Authority

Now, this year, we'll have a woman bishop. Next year, we'll delete a book or two from the New Testament, and we'll certainly get rid of that awkward Old Testament. Then, perhaps, we can go on and change the sacramental elements and adopt the lay presidency of the Eucharist. That, my friends, is not "dispersed authority." It is wholly confused and sectarian authority!

And in all this, never mind the Orthodox and the Roman Catholics. After all, they constitute no more than two-thirds, at least, of Christ's Church Militant here on earth. And never mind the divine imperative to unity and to do nothing deliberately to frustrate it. We can do wholly as we choose. And the reception of our action will make it dogmatically proper and acceptable.

But since all such action is provisional, if Eames and company are to be believed, any sacraments can only be tentative. And thus, without assurance or certitude, and as a layman, I say, "Of what help are such?" In any event, as the Bishop of London has noted, and I dare to reinforce it, without extraordinary verbal dexterity, how do you apply the notion of reception to a "definitive sacramental act," which is either done validly or it is not done at all?

But, of course, verbal dexterity is not lacking. We talk of "impaired communion," blessed phrase! Well, what we mean is "broken communion"—that's what we mean. We appeal to "experience," when what we mean, of course, is that which feels true for me—that's "experience." And, moreover, when plain English proves difficult or even less precision is called for, the laity are treated to wholly subjective doses of *koinonia, diaconia, laos, ekklesia, metanoia!*

Development and Tradition

And, of course, we allow John Henry Newman and the whole notion of development to be wholly hijacked. But not all development is good. And certainly when Newman said that to be perfect is to have changed often, he didn't have in mind changes of secular or ecclesiastical fashion but the change of the Christian heart, and that is *metanoia* indeed!

We do, indeed, have a living, dynamic faith. The Spirit is with us. Tradition *is* a living thing: it's not nostalgia; it's not corruption; it's not a dead hand. But only those who are firmly rooted in the past can go forward confidently to conquer the future. And as we go forth, the truth does not grow, but we grow into it, to quote E.J. Bicknell, whose work on the Thirty-nine Articles may well still be in the memory of some from theological seminary days.

But the same road now lies before us, both for the Church of England and this Episcopal Synod of America. You've had ten years more experience, bitter experience, than we in England have had of the major affliction that besets us. And we can only praise you and thank God for the way in which you have responded to that which, in many places, has been nothing less than persecution and rejection.

But I hope, even so, that if you pass Resolution A [see appendix 5] or something like it, you will go forward with a high confidence and not with pained resignation. Let me assure you that in the Church of England, we expect to win! And we are working to win, and you won't achieve it without working! We are working to defeat the draft legislation to allow the ordination of women put in front of us, and there is *no possibility* of the present synod passing that particular legislation. And we shall be fighting—and I mean fighting—next year to ensure that the new synod, which has then to be elected for another five-year term, is no less determined in its opposition. And, certainly, episcopal support for the proposal, though still strong, is lower than it has been for ten years.

Resolution A

My Lord Chairman, it's a great pleasure for me, as a visitor, to have the opportunity of speaking. I thank you for that high privilege on behalf of my fellow Church of England visitors. It would not be proper for me to comment in detail on your resolution. But I hope you will allow me to say how much I welcome its clarity, its boldness, and its measured concern to act to the limit wholly within the Episcopal Church and to seek for you a loving and positive recognition as an undoubted part of that Church, with an undoubted and unqualified future—that is to say, a future that is not subject to any phasing out or degrading time limits.

Now, all that, I believe, is good and right and true. But of course, there has to be a punch line. For if all that fails—and every effort must be made to see that it does not—it must be clear to all, and clear from the outset, as the president of this synod so properly and so forcefully demonstrated yesterday, that in the last analysis, loyalty to the One Holy Catholic and Apostolic Church as you have received it in this land must prevail and must be safeguarded for the future.

Accordingly, in my respectful opinion, the last paragraph of your resolution properly makes provision—not provocatively, not as an inflammatory act, but faithfully and fairly—for direct action by the bishops of this Episcopal synod with your wholehearted support, action, in loving obedience and loyalty to Christ the King, the only head of his One Holy Church. At the end of the day, we, Church of England and Episcopalians alike, have to choose. Whether in the words of Elijah or John Henry Newman, the substance of the question remains the same: Upon what grounds do you stand, O presbyters, bishops, and laity of the Episcopal Church of the United States of America, whose guests today we are so happy and grateful to be? Thank you.

The Voice of the Wider Communion
The Right Reverend John Hazlewood
Bishop of Ballarat
(Anglican Church of Australia)

It's rather amusing having an Anglican Church "down under," because for nearly one thousand five hundred years, it was supposed to be hell. And, indeed, history tells us that our British forbears made sure it was. There were a very large number of Irish convicts and Scots. With that as a kind of encouragement, the government of the day in Great Britain sent out chaplains—Church of England, of course—and they weren't an enormous success with the imprisoned congregations.

When the "enlightenment" came, and people who were free were able to come to Australia, we always had to put up with American freebooters who chased away most of our whales. But they weren't potential Anglicans, so it didn't matter. We have now grown to a church of four million people, and we have twenty-five bishops to care for them. That's why I've got so much time to come to Fort Worth.

This New Thing

I do thank you very much for your invitation. I thank you for what is happening. I am looking forward to going back "down under" and telling them there about this new thing that is lighting up the enthusiasm of the saints: the old faith, which is given to us and for which we are thankful and to which we must give our lives. Nothing less will do.

In the last few years—actually it almost coincides, not only with Bishop Leonard's consecration, but the year when I gave up teaching theology in a theological school—it all seems to have started going wrong. In my diocese, I have twelve men training for the sacred ministry and about another twelve we call postulants, who have to do so. But where can they be trained? For the theological schools have been taken over by this new kind of theology, which seems to begin from one's rather kindergarten experiences and goes on to the geriatric ones. It doesn't seem to have an order and a discipline and a logic that we used to know in our schools.

I think that the discouragement of philosophy as a background to theology is one of the reasons for this, but I don't wish to go into that deeply. It is a problem for an ordinary Anglican diocese in Australia to find a place to train its clergy. We are trying all sorts of experiments in this matter, and we still have to have them back almost every fortnight to see what they've picked up!

Now, there is one thing I do want to say here, that I have said frequently in Australia: In all the hurly-burly and all the bustle and in all the battling, all the arguing and all the persuading, in all the counting up of numbers as we proceed to restore the great faith that we have been given, the sort of thing that the Evangelical and Oxford movements sought to do in the last century is the sort of thing for us. We must, however, be unlike them in our attitude to those with whom we differ. Let us not talk too much about being in communion here and not there and with somebody and not somebody else.

Let us try to hold in our heart that we are dwelling together, friend and foe, high and low, liberal and tough, in Christ. In Christ, who is our hope; Christ, who is our Savior; Christ, whose Body is stretched across the world in all different kinds, agony and joy: in him we shall all be made alive. And that forever. I believe that if we keep that in mind, as we go about our very proper business of tidying up the mess that's been left in the kitchen from our over-zealous adolescents playing there, we must never forget that we reach out in love and kindness to them.

Archbishop Robinson's Greeting

And I want to finish with some words that Archbishop Donald Robinson asked me to bring. He says,

> This is not a minor or a sectarian dispute. The character of the Christian faith is involved, for we must declare whether our witness to the world, our witness concerning God's sovereign and saving grace, is based on His Divine Revelation contained in Holy Scripture, or not. We dare not allow the spirit of the Age, which is the spirit of relativism, to direct our course. We must be guided by the Mind of Christ, as He has revealed it to His holy apostles and prophets through the Spirit of God.

And his prayer for this meeting is, "May God grant you, and to all of us, a spirit of prayer and intercession as we implore Him to save His People and bless His heritage."

Address: The Beauty of Holiness in the Vineyard of God
The Reverend Dr. William Ralston, Jr.

I take very kindly the invitation to address this synod. I have not been nor am I now a member of ECM, and my ties with the Prayer Book Society ended eight years ago. I am one of the many priests who, with their congregations, are trying to find their way out there within the present deconstruction and disorder of the Episcopal Church. I certainly do not claim to speak for them or represent them, but equally certainly I am one of them.

I think it is important to say this because the fathers of this synod have made it one of their first priorities to reach out to those of us who are not, so to speak, within their immediate circle, in order to offer us comfort and hope. Nothing could be more important or significant about this synod than that.

Isaiah's Song of the Vineyard

The finest poem and the definitive parable of the Kingdom of God in the Old Testament is Isaiah's song of the vineyard (Isaiah 5, KJV). The poem reaches back in recollection to the garden of innocence in which human life was created.

It recalls the giving to us, by the Lord of the garden, our stewardship over his garden and its creatures. It then suggests the further work of God in bringing Israel out of Egypt, providing it a place and a king to oversee it. One of the psalms later makes this explicit: "Thou hast brought a vine out of Egypt . . . and planted it . . . and did cause it to take deep root, and it filled the land" (Ps. 80:8–9, KJV). The poem of Isaiah alludes to all these things. Its associative power is unequaled in Old Testament literature.

So, too, is its spiritual clarity and ethical purity. It begins with the most moving of all poetic invocations:

Now will I sing to my well-beloved
a song of my beloved touching his vineyard.

The poet, Isaiah of Jerusalem, has been given by God, the Lord of the vineyard, a song of the vineyard he will sing back to the author of it. We are, therefore, enabled to be the auditors of a divine poem. God is the Lord both of the vineyard and of the song about it. He is himself the muse of this poem concerning his own work.

Isaiah begins in a bardic tradition as old as poetry itself:

My beloved hath a vineyard in a very fruitful hill:
And he fenced it,
   and gathered out the stones thereof,
   and planted it with the choicest vine,
   and built a tower in the midst of it,
   and also made a winepress therein;
And he looked that it should bring forth grapes,
And it brought forth wild grapes.

Just as with the aboriginal sin in the primal garden, the result of all God's care and provision is nonetheless something unnatural and wild. I do not suppose the dual and perverse qualities of sin have ever been more acutely delimited. Sin is a mode of existence not just against nature, but wild; not just perverse and incoherent, but untamed and desperate.

Judge betwixt Me and My Vineyard

Then God speaks directly. The whole poem is itself a divine utterance, so the voice of God in direct discourse within the indirect discourse of the poem is a literary masterstroke without precedent.

And now, O inhabitants of Jerusalem and men of Judah,
   judge, I pray you, betwixt me and my vineyard,
What could have been done more to my vineyard,
   that I have not done in it?
Wherefore, when I looked that it should bring forth grapes,
   brought it forth wild grapes

This second stanza of the poem is the crux of it. We are invited to use our minds to try to answer God's questions. God does not judge human beings without reason or apart from it. We have here the beginning of a tradition that is still with us in the reproaches read on Good Friday. What can be the cause of so wild and unnatural a thing as the fruit of this vineyard or of the cross of Christ?

The answer is left for a moment in the dark. The actual process of judgment is at work and before us. It begins with an ominous echo of the bardic introduction to the poem as a whole.

And now go to;
I will tell you what I will do to my vineyard:
I will take away the hedge thereof,
   and it shall be eaten up;
   and break down the wall thereof,
   and it shall be trodden down: and
I will lay it waste:
   it shall not be pruned, nor digged,
   but there shall come up briars and thorns:
I will also command the clouds
   that they rain no rain upon it.

Earth, air, fire, and water—all the basic elements are summoned against the wild and unnatural place, and the feet of men and beasts shall trample it in the dust.

The Pain of Speaking Inspired Truth

Then the poet speaks to interpret the song, lest there be any possible misunderstanding of its meaning. We must remember that this is the poet of "unclean lips," dwelling in the midst of "a people of unclean lips," whose eyes had yet been unshackled in the midst of the Temple to see the King, the Lord of hosts, throned among the cherubim in clouds of glory and incense, the Holy One whom he now addresses as "my beloved." Isaiah's eyes are open and his lips burned clean by divine fire. Never has the pain of speaking inspired truth been made so palpable.

For the vineyard of the Lord of hosts
   is the house of Israel,
And the men of Judah
   his pleasant plant.
And he looked for judgment,
   but behold oppression;
For righteousness,
   but behold a cry.

The reason for such destruction is revealed as a spiritual and ethical contradiction. The vineyard exists in violation of the nature of God's power. It has destroyed itself, and the judgement is given as a description of what is happening as a result of this violation, not as some arbitrary determination of divine will. The stunning things, and the juxtaposition so difficult and profound that we still do not comprehend, is that power, the very basic energy of God himself, is righteous in its nature and in its operation.

Plato, himself no mean prophet and poet, declared that being and goodness were intrinsic to each other. Matthew Arnold, considering both this and the Hebraic tradition, declared that God was the "power that makes for righteousness." There is more to be said than that, but that is very well said.

The important thing is to see that, in the last lines of this poem, judgment is a positive fact, an instrument of truth. Its moral and spiritual opposite is oppression.

Behold a Cry

But it is the final line of the poem that takes us away. The Lord looks for righteousness, the natural and orderly result of his grace and governance: "but behold a cry." The measure of Isaiah's ethical and spiritual imagination is in the last two words: "a cry." It is not just "the heavy and the weary weight of all this unintelligible world," though it is this. It is not just the sheer overwhelming mass of human suffering taken as a whole, though it is also this.

It is the terrible individual cry of pain, the cry of each one of us who has suffered or had done unrighteousness. The cry that goes up to God is singular, though how much of the whole content of experienced evil it embodies varies with each one of us. We hold that in the one cry of one particular person—"My God, my God, why hast thou forsaken me?"—the whole weight of the sin that oppresses each of us and all of us together was once for all embodied and made articulate. The beginnings of such an understanding are in this poem of Isaiah, eight hundred years before.

The Substance of Beauty Is Holiness

We are now nearly three millenia away from Isaiah and almost two from the time of our Lord. What can we say today of that part of God's vineyard that is our own Episcopal Church? The premise of all I will attempt to say is in Isaiah's poem.

The substance of beauty in the life of the Church, the vineyard of God, is holiness. The holiness of beauty is a correlate of this but is another topic, something belonging to the sacramental theology of aesthetics.

The peculiar quality of whatever intrinsic beauty the Church possesses is holiness. We are not Puritans, nor do we consider the properties of great beauty in architecture, in music, in painting and sculpture and glass, in language, and in liturgy anything other than signs and intimations of that immortal and imperishable radiance of heaven which, in God's name, we trust and hope will one day open upon our eyes and ears.

But these are not the essential properties of the beauty of the Church. That beauty is her holiness and her righteousness. Her endowment is the judgment of truth, brought to bear by her life in the world upon everything idle, corrupt, wild, disgraceful, and unnatural. This particular beauty is her proper element.

We are, emotionally and spiritually, a long way from the seventeenth century. But it is an apologist for the Church of England in that era (1662) who makes the connection for us between Isaiah and ourselves. In a famous letter, part of which is the most celebrated and certainly the most quotable passage of forensic apologetics ever written, Simon Patrick, later bishop of Ely, speaks of his Church.

"There are," he says, "few men so abstractedly intellectual but that their devotion had need to be advanced with something that may strike upon their outward senses and engage their affections; and therefore, while we live in this region of mortality, we must make use of such external helps, and recommend religion to the people by those ornaments which the Church hath according to her prudence thought fittest for those ends." If one were going to discuss theological aesthetics, this is the place to begin.

The passage continues:

> The Church of Rome is a luxuriant vine, full of superfluous branches and overrun with wild grapes, from whence many a poisonous and intoxicating potion is pressed forth; but the greatest part of the Reformers have done like the rude Thracian in the apologue who, instead of moderate pruning and dressing his vines, as his more skillful Athenian neighbors did, cut them up by the roots. But the Church of England is the only well-ordered vineyard.

A Boast Not Far from the Truth

Today we wince at the epic boast inhering in these gorgeous words. And yet they were not far from the truth and until almost yesterday were still able to be read without fear. They were written in a time when the clergy of the English Church were called stupor mundi: the wonder of the world. Behind them lay the church of Cranmer and Whitgift, of Hooker and Lancelot Andrewes; of Queen Elizabeth and Shakespeare and John Donne.

About them lay the church of Archbishop Laud; of George Herbert and John Cosin; of the Cambridge Platonists; of Jeremy Taylor and Robert Sanderson; of Nicholas Ferrar and Little Gidding. Nor should we forget that this was a time of war and deprivation; of forbidding the liturgy of the Book of Common Prayer; of execution and exile. Yet to come was the church of Thomas Ken and William Law; of Joseph Butler and Samuel Johnson and Christopher Smart; of Thomas Bray and the Wesleys; of Jane Austen and William Blake.

"Let us now praise famous men and our fathers that begat us." But time would fail to tell them all. Their names are magical and incantatory, not just in the moment of glory of the English church, but in our long tradition: David and Patrick; Columba and Aidan and Hilda; Alfred and Dunstan and Alphege; Margaret and Anselm and Becket and Chaucer.

The line has not ceased, and there remain throughout the Church the names of those we call "worthy." We are not given to the making of ecstatic or exotic saints, but holy lives are not the exclusive property of any single branch of the vine of Christ. We can never have too many souls of holy beauty, but our share has been a gracious plenty.

In the generation preceding ours, I doubt if there ever has been a greater outpouring of the love of God with the mind—the rational imagination consecrated to the things of God. A church that can number an Underhill, a Taylor, a Temple, a Lewis, a Sayers, a Williams, an Eliot in a single half-century is not yet bereft of the beauty of holiness. Nor is a church suffering martyrdom bereft of heroes. Only one story, the life of our church in Uganda, would suffice for this.

We live still amidst inherited splendors. The vineyard that is our particular inheritance in the great Catholic Church of which we are (or have been) a part has not failed as a whole. We have also in our own branch of the Church a calendar of the righteous and devout: we can speak of White and Seabury, of Hobart and Huntington and Schereschewsky and Du Bose, of Muhlenberg and Kemper and Brent and the Tuckers. And there remain among us those whose spiritual salt has not lost its savor.

Is Our Branch Diseased?

But the troublesome question remains: Is our particular branch of the Church diseased? No sane person looking at the Episcopal Church as it exists at this moment would dare speak of it as "a well-ordered vineyard," let alone "a school of Christ." What has happened to lay waste the once great beauty of the Episcopal Church—its holy prayers; its steadfast devotion; its fidelity to the revelation with which God has entrusted us; the austere but humane discipline of Christ our Lord? Neither the number of defections from her fellowship nor the ever-increasing financial opulence that is supposed to weigh against this depreciation of members: neither of these criteria is finally of any substance. Both are secular. The substance of the Church, its beauty in the sight of God, is righteousness. Can we honestly look at the Episcopal Church and discern in her the beauty of holiness? Are we weighed in the balance and found wanting?

I want to read you another poem, written last year by a young woman (Diann Blakely Shoaf), a recent graduate of Sewanee. It is entitled "Leaving the Church."

I had wanted stern words, the harsh prayers
of penance. After all, it's Good Friday,
a day of remembrance, remorse, I know
no one here, I finger the pew-seat's worn plush.

I've forgotten my glasses, cannot make out
the hymns. There is no stained glass,
the long windows are shuttered for warmth.
All's stark as New England, the result of a palette

too taken with snow. But how lavish this love
for restraint, the controlled!—there's a surfeit
of white here, both inside and out, too little
to dazzle the eye. Confirmed among incense,

I want colors to covet, stone emblems of glory,
carved doom. And I miss the old tenses,
the firm "Thees" and "Thous";
I want to be stricken, my soul shown

all it lacks. (The new prayer-book will have us
"pass peace" at midpoint, the priest never once
turns his back.) The music
has stopped, he raises his voice, and I'm awed

by old cadence—resonant, ponderous,
slow. He announces the lessons;
a Nobel-winner's short story. Half ashamed
half-alarmed—will a thunderbolt strike?—

I kneel, say a prayer, turn to go.

What Our Churches Really Are

Aristotle reminds us that poetry is more philosophical—of a higher order of truth—than history, and his dictum leads us to remember what our churches really are. They are primarily meant to be places where, when we enter them, we recognize what T.S. Eliot had said of various corners of this earth: "places where prayer has been valid." They are not meetinghouses, nor are they social service centers or occasions for dialogue and entertainment.

They are doors between their own imperfect symbols and the realized glory of God's eternal Kingdom. They are meant precisely to be "emblems of glory." They should be places that compel you to prayer. I remember a visit to a sacred space that was my spiritual home for five blessed years: every day the offices and the Holy Communion, meditations and prayers, penitence and song. I returned to it once again, twenty years later. It looked dusty and uncared for. The altar had been moved to a more fashionable place, and homemade banners of flannel with the slogans of the moment were hung round the walls.

I am not as religious as the young poet whose work I have just read. I did not kneel, could not pray, and left, speechless with sorrow.

O Let Us Live

And yet, what seemed to me desecration and the felt absence of glory was for others the spiritual advance of Christ's religion into the actual milieu of her present existence. Here, I think, we come to a parting of the ways.

The great commentary on Isaiah's song of the vineyard is in the psalm to which I referred earlier. The poet sees the desolation of another age and asks the question, "Why hast thou then broken down her hedge, that all they that go by pluck off her grapes?" And his prayer is, "Turn thee again, thou God of hosts, look down from heaven, behold, and visit this vine. . . ." And finally, in deepest distress at what is for him a matter of life and death: "And so will not we go back from thee: O let us live, and we shall call upon thy Name. Turn us again, O Lord of hosts; show the light of thy countenance, and we shall be whole."

As one reads this psalm, especially with Isaiah's great poem in one's mind, it becomes clear that the destruction described in Isaiah as the direct activity of God has here become the activity, allowed by God, of some enemy: "the wild boar out of the wood doth root it up, and the wild beasts of the field devour it." The metaphors chosen are identical with those of Isaiah. The devastating, magisterial conclusion of Isaiah is turned into the prayer of the later poet. The substance of his prayer is a plea for conversion and wholeness of life. The condition of it is that God would once again "show the light of his countenance."

I have spent time with the song of the vineyard in Isaiah and with this psalm, not only because of their intrinsic magnificence, but because I still believe that to search the Scripture is to find oneself again, to "come to oneself" in the light of God's countenance.

The Episcopal Church: The Wild Vineyard

I am forced to say that I think the present Episcopal Church, as represented by her chief officers and ruling clergy, is Isaiah's wild vineyard, preyed upon by wild boars and beasts. I know, as you know, that everywhere in our Church, scattered in every place, are devout clergy and laity, faithful to the truth that is in Jesus and attempting with godly courage the Christian way. A great many of them are not here and would not think of being represented here, but one hopes and trusts that some such are also, indeed, present here. All these constitute whatever beauty of holiness remains for our Church.

The mysterious and troubling difference for us is that the enemies of the vineyard in our day are ourselves—those of us who have watched the erosion, with eyes that saw not and ears that would not hear; and those who actively have caused it. Our enemies are within our gates, victims of the same spiritual pride and self-imposed cynicism that caused Ahaz to respond to Isaiah's challenge: "I will not ask, neither will I tempt the Lord." The last voice wanted or expected to be heard is the voice of the Lord of the garden.

The poem by the young Episcopalian that I read is a diagnosis of the real disease. Despite our reformed liturgies, despite our advanced sociology and neon-lit sexual sophistication, despite our boasts of compassion and equality, our Church is, as an institution, a spiritual desert, a vineyard wild and spoiled with sin, a temple from which the beauty of holiness has, as in the vision of God's glory seen by Daniel, departed into the clouds.

We must be honest about this. Even in what we now consider the greatest days of our Church, a poet (Sir Walter Raleigh) could look at it out of his prison and write: "Say to the Church it speaks of good, and does no good . . . [and if] the Church reply, then give [the Church] the lie." The Church has never been pure.

But our lie is in the soul: the pride of mind, the alienated will, the corrupted heart. Whether or not it is God's intent to destroy the Episcopal Church is beyond any human power of discernment, but we can surely see that it has become as Hamlet's Denmark: "an unweeded garden, that grows to seed," possessed by things "rank and gross in nature." The very last quality anyone would ascribe to the Episcopal Church is "the beauty of holiness."

To Love the Church Our Mother

And yet, she is our spiritual mother, our home for four centuries, and behind those four the sixteen that lead us back to Glastonbury and to St. Alban. To love the Church as she exists sacramentally in her time and place has ever been our way to learn to love and long for the eternal City of God, which the Church Militant here in earth has always imperfectly represented.

That eternal city measures this, our worldly embodiment of herself. Her measure is holiness and truth. There is no Christian love, nor Christian unity, nor Christian peace, apart from the truth and the beauty of holiness. Without that truthful charity, all our doings, here in Fort Worth or anywhere else, will be "nothing worth."

There is a thanksgiving from the lovely collection of prayers "after the third collect," and it is this, I think, that gives us what we must always remember.

> *God, whom the glorious companies of the redeemed adore,*
> *assembled from all times and places of thy dominion:*
> *We praise thee for the saints of our own communion who*
> *stand before thee, and for the many lamps their holiness hath lit;*
> *And beseech thee that we also may be numbered at the last*
> *with them that have loved thy will and declared thy righteousness;*
> *through Jesus Christ our Lord, who liveth and reigneth*
> *with Thee and the Holy Ghost, one God, world without end.*

Christ the True Vine

But the final word, and the best word is this:

> I am the true vine, and my Father is the husbandman. Every branch in me that beareth not fruit he taketh away: and every branch that beareth fruit, he purgeth it, that it may bring forth more fruit. . . . As the branch cannot bear fruit of itself, except it abide in the vine; no more can ye, except ye abide in me. I am the vine, ye are the branches. . . . Without me ye can do nothing. If a man abide not in me, he is cast forth as a branch, and is withered; and men gather them, and cast them into the fire, and they are burned. . . . Herein is my Father glorified, that ye bear much fruit; so shall ye be my disciples (John 15:1ff., KJV).

Sermon at Evensong
The Reverend Canon Christopher Colven

I have the privilege of being the Master of the Society of the Holy Cross. For those of you unfamiliar with that fraternity, we are a group of nearly a thousand priests and bishops throughout the Communion, two hundred of them here in America.

I want to begin by pledging the prayer and the support of the priests of our society to you here in this synod. In the coming weeks, there will be times of isolation, and I want you to remember then that there are hundreds of us, priests throughout the Communion who are in communion with you, who will be raising you up at our altars day by day.

In the name of the Father and of the Son and of the Holy Spirit. Amen.

Last Sunday afternoon an old man found his way into the Shrine of Our Lady at Walsingham, and for an hour, without a single note, he held a congregation of several hundred spellbound. He was the Belgian Cardinal Suenens, one of the formative influences on the Second Vatican Council.

Some time ago, Cardinal Suenens gave an interview in which he was asked the question, "Why are you a man of hope, despite the confusion in which we find ourselves today?" I think it's worth giving you part of this reply:

> I am a man of hope, not for human reasons, nor from any natural optimism, but because I believe the Holy Spirit is at work in the Church and in the world, even where His Name remains unheard. I am an optimist because I believe the Holy Spirit is the spirit of creation. To those who welcome Him, He gives each day fresh liberty and renewed joy and trust. The long history of the Church is filled with the wonders of the Holy Spirit. Think only of the prophets and

saints, who, in times of darkness, have discovered a spring of grace and shed beams of light upon our path. I believe in the surprises of the Holy Spirit. Who would dare to say that the love and imagination of God were exhausted. To hope is a duty, not a luxury. To hope is not to dream, but to turn dreams into reality. Happy are those who dream dreams and are ready to pay the price to make them come true.

Hope Is a Duty

The substance of what I want to say to you is that, in Cardinal Suenens' words, "to hope, for a Christian, is a duty, not a luxury." This message of hope is not based on human reasoning or on natural optimism but on the Word of God. So, together, let us look at what the Spirit is saying to us, in the scriptures we've heard this afternoon.

First, there was Ezekiel's vision of the Valley of Dry Bones. Note how it begins: "The hand of the Lord was laid upon me." This is no daydream of Ezekiel's own imagining; he isn't fantasizing. This is no wishful thinking. The initiative comes from God himself. What does God show to his prophet? Israel—lifeless, desiccated, all dried up, empty, with nothing left to offer. And Ezekiel is commanded to take the initiative. Prophesy to the dry bones, God tells him. He does so. They begin to cohere. Again, God tells Ezekiel, breathe on these dead bones. Let them live. He does so, with the result that they came to life again and stood up on their feet, a great and immense army.

As I stand here with the authority to preach, the significance of that vision for this synod seems all too clear. It may sound arrogant as I say it, but nonetheless, I believe it to be the truth: We are those who have been entrusted with the message of life. We are those who have not compromised the revealed truth about Jesus Christ. And we are those who remain faithful to the convenanted channels of God's grace. With Ezekiel, we, too, can truly claim that the hand of the Lord is upon us. Therefore, like Ezekiel, we have a unique responsibility to prophesy.

And the Valley of Dry Bones—what and where is that? How shall we define it? One answer would be to say that the "valley" is a depressingly apt description of a Church that no longer stands under the judgment of the gospel, a Church whose agenda is determined by contemporary pressures alone. But that would be too obvious and too narrow. The Valley of Dry Bones is surely the whole of Western secularized society, far away from its spiritual roots, of which the United States of America and ECUSA are but parts. The challenge of Ezekiel's vision is to the whole Catholic Church, that it will recognize itself as the unique vehicle of truth down through the ages and that in that recognition it may revive its own confidence in its power to proclaim.

The Enemy Relativism

As we've already been reminded several times, the great enemy today is relativism. All too easily, we are fooled into accepting that ours is only one voice among many, that any one view has equal validity with any other. That's not a view that Athanasius would have understood, thank God. Ezekiel did not prophesy in his own strength. He was fulfilling a mandate he had received from the Lord. Power attached to what Ezekiel said, simply because he became the effective sign of God's will to salvation. We, too, must have confidence in the gospel we proclaim, quite simply, because we are Catholic Christians. And it is God's good news, not ours, that we are *mandated*, that we are *emboldened,* to speak.

But what is that gospel? Our second lesson is quite clear on that score. Peter and John are arrested in the Temple for preaching the resurrection of Jesus. They've run up against the religious establishment of their own day, and they're hauled before the council and interrogated. Here they are: two of the little people, confronted by intellect and influence and power. One would have expected them to be over-awed, cowed. But not at all. For Peter, like Ezekiel before him, is filled with the Holy Spirit. He witnesses to his own conviction of the resurrection. He talks to them of Jesus, and he says, "For of all names in the world given to men, this is the only one by which we can be saved."

Here this afternoon, do we honestly believe that? For this, and this alone, is where we can take our stand: on the uniqueness of Jesus and his power to save. My brothers and sisters in Christ, this is the sole reason for our meeting here in synod. There can be no other. The only justification for our standing out against much of the tide that prevails within Anglicanism is that we believe it compromises, it sells short, the full stature of Christ. And in obedience to the Holy Spirit, we can do no other than to continue to proclaim a view of Jesus that is authentically catholic, in a way that is truly evangelical. For our struggle is not ultimately about structures or about levels of communion; it is about our obedience to what the Father has chosen to reveal of himself in Jesus.

Peter and John, when bullied, when cajoled, when bribed, when intimidated, could not deny what they had experienced as salvation. And neither, my brothers and sisters, can we. The mystery of faith is ever the same. For Christ has died. Christ is risen. And Christ will come again. For of all the names in the world given to men, this is the only one by which we can be saved. The challenge of this synod to us must first be in terms of personal holiness. For if we are to dare to prophesy to our fellow Anglicans and beyond, we must first feel the breath of life blown into us. And if we are to dare to preach a gospel of salvation, we must first ensure that Jesus is risen and at work in us. The salt that has lost its savor is fit only to be cast out and to be trodden underfoot.

Our Supernatural Hope

Our hope, then, is not a human hope but the utter conviction that, inasmuch as we reflect the truth of God, not even the walls of hell, let alone a General Convention or a local House of Bishops, can prevail against us. As our hope is a supernatural one, so we must not allow our human weaknesses and apprehensions to daunt us. Perhaps, sitting here, we feel we don't have the power to prophesy of Ezekiel or the sheer guts of Peter and John. But each one of us in baptism has a personal vocation to be faithful to God, who reveals himself to me and to you as our loving Father.

I do not know what the immediate future holds. I suspect that, for many of us, there will be a lot of pain and much confusion. But there is no way out. There is no escape route. There is no turning back. For we are committed to the proclamation of what God has shown us in Jesus. As Father Mackonochie, one of the founding fathers of the Society of the Holy Cross, said to the first priests, "Our vocation involves no surrender, no desertion. For we are to dig a pit for the cross, wherever we are." And if we can do that, if we can be faithful to where God has placed us, then we have the right to wait expectantly to be surprised by God.

For "I believe in the surprises of the Holy Spirit. Who would dare to say that the love and imagination of God were exhausted? To hope is a duty, not a luxury. To hope is not to dream, but to turn dreams into reality. Happy are those who dream dreams and are ready to pay the price to make them come true."

Heavenly Father, pour down your Holy Spirit upon your whole Church. Grant us a new vision of your glory, a new experience of your power, a new faithfulness to your Word, a new consecration to your service, that through our renewed witness your holy name may be glorified and your Kingdom advanced. Through Jesus Christ our Lord. AMEN.

Saturday, June 3, 1989

Homily at Morning Prayer
The Reverend Dr. Roger Beckwith

LESSONS: Josh. 1:1–9; 2 Tim. 3:10–4:8.

TEXT: "This Book of the law shall not depart out of thy mouth, but thou shalt meditate therein day and night, that thou mayest observe to do according to all that is written therein: for then thou shalt make thy way prosperous, and then thou shalt have good success. Have not I commanded thee? Be strong and of a good courage: be not affrighted, neither be thou dismayed: for the Lord thy God is with thee whithersoever thou goest" (Josh. 1:8–9, KJV).

We go back this morning even further in the history of the people of God, to the very point of their entry into the Promised Land, after their delivery from slavery in Egypt, after their forty years' wandering in the wilderness, after the revelation of God's Law to them and the making of his covenant—his solemn agreement with them, in which he took them for his people and they took him for their God and promised to obey his Law in the land he would give them.

What Do You Do?

So God addresses Joshua, and the first thing he says is, "Moses my servant is dead" (Josh. 1:2, KJV). What a shattering fact that must have been! What do you do, with no one to lead you? And especially shattering for Joshua. All these years he had been Moses' personal assistant and had done his bidding and had depended upon him for everything. And now Moses was dead. So what do you do? Do you say, Well, it was wonderful while it lasted, but now we might as well shut up shop?

Apparently not! For God continues:

Now therefore arise, go over this Jordan, thou and all this people, unto the land which I do give to them, even to the children of Israel. Every place that the sole of your foot shall tread upon, to you have I given it, as I spoke unto Moses. From the wilderness and this Lebanon, even unto the great river, the river Euphrates, all the land of the Hittites, and unto the great sea toward the going down of the sun, shall be your border. There shall not any man be able to stand before thee all the days of thy life: as I was with Moses, so I will be with thee: I will not fail thee, nor forsake thee. Be strong and of a good courage; for thou shalt cause this people to inherit the land which I swore unto their fathers to give them (Josh. 1:2–6, KJV).

All these years that Joshua had been serving Moses had also been his training to be a leader himself, and God's promise to him was, "As I was with Moses, so I will be with thee. I will *not* fail thee, *nor* forsake thee."

On Your Knees and on Your Feet

It is bad news for the curate when the rector is taken ill or leaves or even dies. It is bad news for the congregation, too. But it is also a time of challenge.

What has the curate been trained for but to take responsibility himself? And what has the congregation been doing in the pews all these years? Has it learned nothing? Can it do nothing? Is there no ministry of the laity? No one capable of learning to read the offices during the vacancy? No one used to teaching children in the Sunday school, who could for once explain the Scriptures to the adults?

It is bad news for the diocese when its bishops retires—at least if you have got this kind of bishop here! But *when* your bishop retires, get down on your knees and then get busy on your feet. "I will *not* fail thee, *nor* forsake thee," says God, and God *never* retires. The ECM bishops are few—we all know that. But the movement that began here this week is not going to shrink; it is going to grow. The soft underbelly of liberalism is as vulnerable as vulnerable can be. This is the Church! And we have allowed it to be taken over by those who certainly love power but know nothing of the power of the gospel.

And then verse 7: "Only be strong and very courageous, to observe to do according to all the Law, which Moses my servant commanded thee: turn not from it to the right hand or to the left, that thou mayest have good success whithersoever thou goest." "Only be strong and very courageous." Not to beat the Canaanites this time: they are the outward enemy, and we do need strength and courage to beat them. But because they are outward, we can see them and get the measure of them and cope with them.

But verse 7 says, "Be strong and very courageous *to observe to do according to all the Law which Moses my servant commanded thee:* turn not from it to the right hand or to the left." These are the inner battles, which are much harder to fight. Obeying a law may sound very straightforward, and in a sense it *is*: the trouble is not with the Law but with us, as we will see if we look at this Law for a minute.

Our Lord told us of the two greatest commandments of the Law ("of the Law," note—he did not invent them himself). The first is Deut. 6:5, KJV, "Thou shalt love the Lord thy God with all thy heart and with all thy soul and with all thy strength." "All"—that's a tall order, isn't it? But that must be our goal. The second like unto it is Lev. 19:18, KJV, "Thou shalt love thy neighbor as thyself." In the Sermon on the Mount, our Lord paraphrased it like this: "Whatsoever things ye would that men should do unto you, even so do unto them, for this is the Law and the Prophets" (Matt. 7:12, KJV). Even so do unto them: again, a difficult demand for fallen humanity.

The Ten Commandments

The Book of the Law is summed up, a little more at large, in the Ten Commandments of Exodus 20 and Deuteronomy 5, which were laid up in the ark of the covenant, in the Holy of Holies, at the very heart of Israel's worship. And what do these say?

1. "Thou shalt have none other gods but me."
2. "Thou shalt not make unto thyself a graven image." We must watch this.
3. "Thou shalt not take the name of the Lord thy God in vain." The great increase in the profane use of the name of God and of our Lord Jesus Christ in English-speaking society over the last twenty years, especially in the media, and even among Christians, has been a very striking fact. Christians must set an example here and protest against wanton examples at every opportunity.
4. "Remember the sabbath day to keep it holy." Like the Jews, we must sanctify one day in seven, if we want to sanctify the whole week.
5. "Honour thy father and thy mother."
6. "Thou shalt do no murder."
7. "Thou shalt not commit adultery." Perhaps I ought to repeat that—thou shalt *not* commit adultery. Our Lord connected divorce with adultery, and in practice, as we know, they are usually mixed up

together. One of the more curious books on my shelves is a book written by the great Bishop Samuel Wilberforce, of Oxford, before he became a bishop. It is entitled *A History of the Protestant Episcopal Church in America*, and it was published at London in 1844. It gives high praise to the Episcopal Church, but it ends with two points of criticism. One is that some of its bishops are slave-owners, in the North as well as in the South. And the other is this: "To divorce his wife, or even to fail in the attempt . . . would not greatly impair the reputation, even of one in holy orders" (p. 409ff). So, if this one is true, it is an old American custom—now spreading to England as well—and I have been very happy to hear in this synod that you are determined to fight against it.

8. "Thou shalt not steal."
9. "Thou shalt not bear false witness against thy neighbor."
10. "Thou shalt not covet." Short of adultery, short of stealing, there is the coveting that leads to it, and we must check that, too.

No wonder our passage goes on: "This Book of the Law shall not depart out of thy mouth, but thou shalt meditate therein day and night, that thou mayest observe to do according to all that is written therein: for then shalt thou make thy way prosperous, and then thou shalt have good success. Have not I commanded thee? Be strong and of a good courage; be not affrighted, neither be thou dismayed: for the Lord thy God is with thee whithersoever thou goest" (Josh. 1:8–9, KJV). What a privilege to have the Bible, the Word of God, in our hands and to be free to read it, not just on Sunday, but on every day of the week. Let us see that we take advantage of the privilege—not just bishops and clergy, but laity as well.

New Experiences

Many things in this synod have been new experiences to me. And one of them has been that I do not usually have a dozen bishops in the congregation when I preach. You, my fathers in God, are the leaders of the Church. To you above all are God's words of Joshua, the leader of the People of God of those days, addressed. "This Book of the Law shall not depart out of thy mouth, but thou shalt meditate therein day and night, that thou mayest observe to do according to all that is written therein. . . . Be *strong* and of a *good courage;* be not affrighted, neither be thou dismayed: for *the Lord thy God is with thee* whithersoever thou goest."

I do not want to conclude without reminding you that this synod has been called in a very significant year, 1989. This is a great year of anniversaries for Anglicans. It is the 500th anniversary of the birth, in 1489, of Archbishop Thomas Cranmer, who gave us our Prayer Book and our Thirty-nine Articles (or Forty-two Articles, as they were in his time). It is also, I have no need to remind you, the 200th anniversary of the first authorized American Prayer Book, which came out in 1789.

I was so happy that you decided to pass Resolution B yesterday [see appendix 5] and to let the two present American Prayer Books compete on equal terms. That will be the surest way to find out which of the two has the better claim to the loyalty of American Anglicans.

I have no wish to anticipate that decision, but I am bound to say that I am very disturbed by the revolutionary character of many of the new service books that have appeared across the Anglican Communion since the later 1960s. To tear the theological and devotional heart out of Cranmer's liturgy and to give the Church back a shell, as has been done in some countries, shows small appreciation of our liturgical heritage and small love for the Church.

The Nonjurors

But 1989 is also a third anniversary. It is the 300th anniversary of 1689, when eight bishops of the Church of England, including William Sancroft, then Archbishop of Canterbury, decided that they could not in good conscience take the oath of allegiance to William and Mary, while the previous monarch James II, to whom they had already sworn allegiance, was still alive.

They had no sympathy with James II's attempt to make the Church of England Roman Catholic: indeed, five of them had been among the seven bishops whom James had committed to the Tower of London for resisting that attempt. In churchmanship they were old-fashioned High Churchmen, strongly Protestant and Prayer Book in their sympathies, like the Protestant Episcopal Church of pre-Tractarian days. (Perhaps you have learned better since—I pass no judgment on that.)

But it is not their churchmanship that matters: what matters is their courageous determination to obey their conscience, come what may. As a result, they were first suspended, and two years later they were deprived of their sees. Was that failure? No indeed. Because of their witness, the Anglican Church has never been quite the same since. And it is in their footsteps that our bishops and ourselves are called to tread today.

We are called to do the right, come what may. And may God defend the right. AMEN.

Sermon at the Closing Eucharist
The Right Reverend Clarence C. Pope, Jr.

". . . that they may all be one; even as thou, Father, art in me, and I in thee . . ." (John 17:21, KJV).

The Gospel we have just heard read contains our Lord's great high priestly prayer, a prayer that must not be lost on us. The circumstances under which we have gathered these few days might overshadow and tend to lessen our vision of the great Church as we take necessary action to hold and extend our mission.

And yet it is precisely because of our concern for unity with the Church that we have met in such an extraordinary way. Our concern extends not only to those who have remained faithful to what we believe to be essential, that is, to the given revelation of God in Holy Scripture and historic tradition, but also to those who disagree with us in fundamental ways.

Our Vocation

Ours is not a vocation to smugness and insularity but to a holy witness that reaches out to the world, holding Christ high that all might be drawn to him. In particular, if we are faithful to our Lord's great prayer, we must not forget consideration for members of our own Anglican family who do not share our beliefs and convictions about faith and order. Charity, courtesy, and forbearance must be the rule and not the exception.

We must also remember those other Anglicans who, for the present, are not in communion with the See of Canterbury but who hold the faith in common with us. We must pray and work diligently that reunion with them might be realized as soon as possible.

And yet our concern cannot stop there, because ours is a mission that reflects that of the Church universal in her quest for the redemption of all mankind. Ours is a loyalty we must claim to be of a higher order than to any institution and that is to the Church Catholic, "universal, holding earnestly the Faith for all time, in all countries, and for all people" ("Offices of Instruction," 1928 Prayer Book). Or to put it another way: "the whole faith to all people" ("Catechism," 1979 Prayer Book).

We can do none of this if we lose sight of who we are—if we become amnesic and lose sight of all we claim for ourselves and for our mission. Stressful times are the devil's workshop and we must be on our guard to remember always, even as our forebears of old sat and wept when they remembered.

Remembering

But let me hasten to say that I am not so concerned about weeping as I am about remembering: "By the waters of Babylon, there we sat down and wept, when we remembered Zion. On the willows, there we hung up our lyres. For there our captors required of us songs, and our tormentors, mirth, saying, 'Sing us one of the songs of Zion.' How shall we sing the Lord's song in a foreign land?" (Ps. 137:1–4, RSV).

Memory is a wonderful faculty, and in the portion of the psalter I just read there is evidence of a remembered remembrance. The past tense of the verbs in the first three verses indicate the psalmist was writing of the past event in which the remembrance of grander times was very painful to his fellow religionists.

These Jews were in captivity and far removed from Zion—Jerusalem—and all that that meant to them. Their memory served to remind them of who they were in spite of their sadness and would ultimately be the instrument of their salvation. It would not be very difficult for those of us gathered here to think of ourselves in those poetically sad words of Psalm 137. We have all sat down and wept as we remembered our own Zion before the capture—before a tireless and demanding secularism began its stifling effect upon the Church in this country.

One has to wonder what happened to those who no longer weep with us—or those who now seem happy with their captivity. What has happened to their memory? St. Augustine, in his work *On the Trinity*, wrote, "We know many things which in some sense live by memory, and so in some sense die by being forgotten."

Being and Doing Church

But we are not here to weep and wring our hands anymore—we are here to remember and because of that memory to get on with the job of being and doing Church in the sense of the givens of Holy Scripture and the received tradition.

I think St. Paul must have had us in mind when in his second letter to Timothy he wrote,

> I charge you in the presence of God and of Christ Jesus who is to judge the living and the dead, and by his appearing and his kingdom: preach the word, be urgent in season and out of season, convince, rebuke, and exhort, be unfailing in patience and in teaching. For the time is coming when people will not endure sound teaching, but having itching ears they will accumulate for themselves teachers to suit their own likings, and will turn away from listening to the truth and wander into myths. As for you, always be steady, endure suffering, do the work of an evangelist, fulfill your ministry. (2 Tim. 4:1–5, RSV).

"Always be steady, endure suffering, do the work of an evangelist, fulfill your ministry." We do this best when we have a holy remembrance—a remembrance stirred by the Holy Spirit to make lively within us the gospel of Jesus Christ. As we receive Holy Communion in a few minutes let us be mindful of the remembrance that brings us the sacramental presence of our Savior. This is the essence of our hope and the source of our strength to accomplish the monumental work ahead of us to which we believe God has called us.

Appendices

Appendix 1.

A Pastoral Letter Convoking a Synod from the Bishops of the Evangelical and Catholic Mission

To the faithful in Christ Jesus in the Episcopal Church and in the Anglican Churches throughout the world: Greetings in the Name of the Holy and Undivided Trinity, Father, Son, and Holy Spirit.

Preamble

1. The final crisis of the Episcopal Church is now upon us. We, as Bishops in the Church of God who exercise our ministry within the Episcopal Church, are deeply aware of the anguish of many of the institution's members over the progressive disintegration of its faithful witness to the Gospel during the past two decades. The recent election for a Suffragan Bishop in the Diocese of Massachusetts is the act which has brought us to the point at which indecision and inaction are no longer options. Bishops are called to care for the whole Church, and this solemn duty now compels us to seek a way in which obedience to the Faith and Order to which Scripture and Tradition bear witness may be continued within this Church. As an institution, the Episcopal Church seems neither able nor willing to provide such a way, so it falls to us, together with clergy and laity of like belief, to make provision. While we are convinced that many of the institutions within what has been known as the Anglican Communion have failed and are failing to uphold the divinely-given Order of the Church, we are equally convinced that the Anglican way of being Christian has not failed and must be preserved, upheld, and propagated.

2. We would strongly urge all who are distressed by recent events to forego precipitate and individualistic reactions, whether as persons or as groups, for we are committed to the enactment of a comprehensive reponse to the crisis, of which this Pastoral Letter is but the first element.

3. We must make clear the principles upon which we are acting; we are convinced that there is a crucial distinction to be made between the God-given Order of the Church and the humanly-invented institutions in the Church. During the history of the Church, her members have found it expedient to set up institutions to assist in maintaining faithful witness to the Gospel. Among these institutions are councils, systems of Church government, canons, forms of liturgical worship, and local assemblies such as General Convention. These institutions exist by Divine permission, not by Divine command. They are not perfect; they may be changed; they are subject to corruption. The distinction between these institutions and the divinely-appointed Order of the Church is often blurred in the minds of the Church's members, but it is a real distinction to which the Anglican doctrine of the Church has borne witness from the time of its classical articulation in the sixteenth century in the Articles of Religion. Its roots stretch back to the origin of Christianity.

4. The Order of the Church to which we refer is a gift from the Father through the Son in the Holy Spirit. It lays claim to the loyalty of all Christians, above and beyond any deviation sanctioned by any humanly-invented institution, whether secular or ecclesiastical. The principles we believe to be the substantial deposit of faith and order committed by Christ and His Apostles to the Church unto the end of the world, and therefore incapable of compromise or surrender are:

(a) The Holy Scriptures of the Old and New Testament, as "containing all things necessary to salvation," and as being the rule and ultimate standard of faith.

(b) The Apostles' Creed, as the Baptismal Symbol; and the Nicene Creed, as the sufficient statement of the Christian faith.

(c) The two Sacraments ordained by Christ Himself—Baptism and the Supper of the Lord—ministered with unfailing use of Christ's words of Institution, and of the elements ordained by Him.

(d) The Historic Episcopate, locally adapted in the methods of its administration to the varying needs of the nations and peoples called of God into the Unity of His Church.

5. Considered as an institution, the Episcopal Church is in rebellion against this Order. The venerable Anglican principle of comprehending nonessentials within the clearly defined doctrinal and moral limits has been replaced in the practice of this institution by a vague and sentimental notion of "inclusivism" which sets at naught the classical Christian standards of belief and behavior. It is ever more evident that the tenderness with which this notion is set forth is but a thin velvet glove sheathing the mailed fist of intolerance.

6. At the root of the present crisis is the rejection of the authority of God's revelation of Himself and His will for humanity in favor of a religiosity tailored to human convenience. This rejection expresses itself in the challenge to the central authority of Holy Scripture, the denial of Jesus Christ as the full, perfect, and sufficient self-revelation of God, the proposals to rewrite the language of the Bible and liturgical prayer to suit humanistic ideologies, the decay of marital discipline, and the pressure to abandon the received standards of chastity, as well as the purported admission of women to priestly and episcopal orders. The institutions of the Episcopal Church have allowed, aided, and encouraged these deviations.

7. When an institution has turned from its original purpose, those who remain faithful to that purpose are obliged to seek the institution's reformation, replacement, or transcendence, as the situation dictates. This must be done in a way which avoids sacrificing any aspect of the Church's Order, preserves the integrity of the Church's witness to God's revelation, and retains within the bond of faith, hope, and charity the greatest number of persons of good will.

8. Our special responsibility as Bishops obliges us to do all that God grants us to do, both spiritually and materially, to secure the continuation of faithful witness within the Episcopal Church to God's Order for the Church. Because we do take seriously our role in the institution in which we serve, we are bound to resist those of its programs and activities which threaten the Church's Faith and Order. We do so without regard to the temporal consequences which might be inflicted upon us. We are prepared to do whatever is necessary to that end, within the institution's regulations if possible, and beyond them if required. We shall spare no effort to minister to all who suffer for their loyalty to the Church's Order and to keep their painful plight before the conscience of the Church and the eyes of all men and women of good will.

Declaration

9. Our convictions bind us to regard the purported admission of women to the episcopate and presbyterate as in itself destructive of communion. Therefore, we must refrain from any and all actions which might signify acceptance of this novelty. There is no certainty that these ministries are or can be what they purport to be. Our communion with persons so ordained and with those ordained by them can only be considered seriously impaired; our relationship with those who have consented to their ordination will be placed in jeopardy. We must also state that we shall not recognize nor be bound by any action of the

Episcopal Church which deprives of office or status any person who holds our position, if such action is based solely or primarily upon objection to the principles we have set forth.

10. From the earliest times, the elders of God's people have been summoned by their leaders in moments of crisis to assemble and take counsel. Therefore we, as a college of Bishops, hereby convoke a Synod of representatives of the clergy and laity holding the convictions that we have declared to meet in the city of Fort Worth, Texas, on June 1–3, 1989. The purpose of this Synod will be to consider how we shall be the Church within the Episcopal Church and to adopt a detailed and unified plan for active witness in the face of the institution's present disintegration. The basis of participation shall be personal subscription to the Declaration appended to this letter. Specific procedures for the organization of the Synod shall be made available by the end of this year.

11. We labor under no illusions about the difficulty of the task to which we have been set, for the forces arrayed against us are strong and determined, and yet we are of good courage. Although the material consequences of continuing faithfully may be heavy for us and for those who stand with us, the spiritual debilitation of further inaction is most sure, and we would not appear empty-handed and ashamed before Him whose Apostolic Commission we bear. May the Lord favor our undertaking with His presence and His power.

The Grace of our Lord Jesus Christ, and the love of God, and the fellowship of the Holy Spirit be with you all evermore. AMEN.

11 November 1988

Appendix 2.
Declaration of Common Faith and Purpose

**In the Name of the Holy and Undivided Trinity:
Father, Son, and Holy Spirit. Amen**

I, _____ , A Lay Member/ Deacon/Priest/Bishop of the One Holy Catholic and Apostolic Church serving God in the Episcopal Church, affirm the following, in common with the Bishops who have declared in their Pastoral Letter of November 11, 1988 their intention to seek a way in which faithful witness to apostolic Faith and Catholic Order may be continued within this Church:

I believe our Lord Jesus Christ has given His Church an Order which claims the loyalty of faithful Christians above and beyond any deviation sanctioned by any humanly-invented institution, whether secular or ecclesiastical.

I accept the Holy Scriptures of the Old and New Testament, as "containing all things necessary to salvation," and as being the rule and ultimate standard of faith and morals.

I accept the Apostles' Creed, as the Baptismal Symbol; and the Nicene Creed as the sufficient statement of the Christian faith.

I accept the two Sacraments ordained by Christ Himself—Baptism and the Supper of the Lord—ministered with unfailing use of Christ's words of Institution, and of the elements ordained by Him.

I accept the Historic Episcopate, locally adapted in the methods of its administration to the varying needs of the nations and peoples called of God into the Unity of His Church; and I do not consider that the churches of the Anglican Communion have authority to change the historic tradition of the Church that the Christian ministerial priesthood is male, and I will refrain from any and all actions which might signify acceptance of such purported change.

I will do what God grants me the strength to accomplish to uphold the Church's Order, both materially and spiritually.

I will resist all present and future attempts to compromise the integrity of this Order, without regard to the temporal consequences that may be inflicted by the Episcopal Church.

I will be guided in this endeavor by the Godly counsel of the Bishops who share this common faith and purpose and of the Synod convoked by them.

In making this Declaration, I accept all the responsibilities which pertain to the common witness of all who participate in this endeavor, and I ask God's blessing upon our labors.

Appendix 3.
Statement of the Synod Gathered in Fort Worth in Response to the Summons of the Bishops of the Evangelical and Catholic Mission

As Bishops, Clergy and Laity of the Episcopal Church, we thank Almighty God for gathering us. We are gratefully conscious of our community with the thousands of North American Anglicans who have signed the "Declaration of Common Faith and Purpose" issued by our bishops and who have joined in the responsibilities of the Christian witness to which we have been summoned. We are aware of the keen interest with which the proceedings of this Synod are being followed by our brothers and sisters throughout the Anglican Communion and beyond. We acknowledge and are strengthened by the support and prayers of Anglicans from the world-wide Communion and ecumenical partners who have gathered with us or have sent messages associating themselves with the task to which we are called.

We affirm in Assembly the "Declaration of Common Faith and Purpose" which unites this Synod and we acknowledge the crisis in the Episcopal Church which occasioned it. Accordingly, we proclaim our Lord Jesus Christ who is the Word Incarnate and who has given a divine order to His Church. We accept the Holy Scriptures of the Old and New Testaments as containing all things necessary to salvation and as being the rule and ultimate standard of faith.

We accept the Apostles' Creed as the Baptismal Symbol, and the Nicene Creed as the sufficient standard of the Christian faith. We accept the two Sacraments ordained by Christ Himself—Baptism and the Supper of the Lord—ministered with unfailing use of Christ's words of Institution, and of the elements ordained by Him. We also accept the Historic Episcopate and our obligation to continue it as the means of handing on the full Faith and Order of the Apostolic Church.

We declare our determination to maintain and propagate this Faith and

Practice according to the patterns of teaching, worship, church order, spiritual and moral life developed by historic Anglicanism, especially in the Books of Common Prayer. We meet to make provision for the mission of those who are united in our common faith and purpose, to increase communion with faithful Anglicans throughout the world, and to resist the destruction of the basis of our common life.

We accept our obligation as inheritors of the Apostolic Faith and Order to resist the replacement of Holy Scripture as the standard of faith, worship, order, and discipline in the Episcopal Church.

In particular we reject endeavors to adopt inclusive language that obscure the Lordship of Christ and the Kingdom of the Father. We reject actions of those in the Episcopal Church who accept fornication, adultery, and homosexual unions as "alternative Christian life-styles."

Affirming the sanctity of life, we oppose abortion on demand and euthanasia.

We affirm the Scriptural and historic standards of faith and morals for admission to the ordained ministry. Since we uphold the historic apostolic ministry, we oppose the breach of two thousand years of unbroken practice of male priesthood and episcopacy. We seek to stop the disintegration of the Anglican Communion. We desire to restore the movement toward ecumenical unity with the historic Catholic churches.

We meet to draw into renewed fellowship those who have been alienated by deviations from the historic faith in the Episcopal Church. We reaffirm our bonds with those who continue faithfully their life in the Church. We intend to take those steps necessary for the mission to which our common faith and purpose summons us. We declare that we shall stand united in the actions necessary to further the vital mission and strengthened communion of Christ's faithful people throughout the world.

The Bishop of Albany	+Victor Rivera, retired
The Bishop of Eau Claire	+Charles T. Gaskell, retired
The Bishop of Fond du Lac	+William C.R. Sheridan, retired
The Bishop of Fort Worth	+Charles F. Boynton, retired
The Bishop of Quincy	+Clarence R. Haden, retired
The Bishop of San Joaquin	+Hal R. Gross, retired
+Stanley Atkins, retired	+William H. Brady, retired
+A. Donald Davies, retired	+James L. Duncan, retired
+Paul Reeves, retired	+Robert H. Mize, Jr., retired

Appendix 4.
Episcopal Synod of America Constitution

PREAMBLE

The Episcopal Synod of America is an Association of Episcopal Dioceses and Congregations, the purposes of which are:
Sharing personal resources and skills
Establishing and implementing cooperative programs
Expressing the mind of the Synod to the National Church in order to strengthen and encourage one another in our common life in Christ and His Church.

ARTICLE I

The Episcopal Synod of America is a voluntary association of Dioceses and Areas committed to upholding Evangelical Faith and Catholic Order in The Episcopal Church, and called to proclaim and propagate this Faith and Order. A Diocese may join the Synod by action of its convention, Standing Committee or Executive Council.

ARTICLE II

Section 1. The legislative body of the Synod shall consist of a House of Bishops and a House of Deputies which shall sit, deliberate and vote together, provided that the two Houses shall vote separately as provided by Constitution or Ordinance. No person shall serve in such legislative body without having first signed the Synod's Declaration of Faith.

Section 2. Every Bishop of the Church having jurisdiction within a Diocese of the Synod, every Bishop Coadjutor, Suffragan Bishop, Assistant Bishop, and every Bishop whose episcopal work has been within the Synod, but who by reason of advanced age or bodily infirmity has resigned, together with all Area Bishops, shall have a seat, voice and vote in the House of Bishops of the Synod.

Section 3. The membership of the House of Deputies shall be as provided by Ordinance. The term of office of a Deputy shall be determined by the Diocese or Area from which the Deputy is elected.

Section 4. There shall be a regular annual meeting of the legislative body of the Synod. Special meetings may be called by the President. Ordinances may be enacted as needed by either a regular or specially called meeting, by majority vote of those present.

ARTICLE III

The officers of the Synod shall be:

a. A President, who may be one of the Bishops, Priests, Deacons or members of the Laity of the Synod elected by the legislative body of the Synod for a three year term.

b. A Vice President, who shall be a Bishop member of the Synod if the President is not and who otherwise may be one of the Priests, Deacons or Laity of the Synod, elected by the legislative body of the Synod for a three year term. If the President is not a Bishop, the Vice President shall serve ex-officio as President of the House of Bishops of the Synod and shall represent the Synod in all matters requiring the participation of a Bishop.

c. A Secretary and Treasurer, elected for a three year term to be elected in years when elections for President and Vice President are not held.

ARTICLE IV

The Synodical Council shall be established by Ordinance.

ARTICLE V

Section 1. Congregations, institutions or organizations located in Dioceses which are not members of the Synod, but which wish to be a part of the Synod, may be grouped into geographical clusters known as Areas. Each Area shall be entitled to representation in the House of Deputies and may participate in Synodical programs on the same basis as a Diocese. Areas shall be designated by either the legislative body of the Synod or by the Synodical Council. A congregation may join an area by vote of its Vestry or at its annual parish meeting, without prejudice to its place within its current Diocese of The Episcopal Church.

Section 2. A Bishop may be designated by the legislative body of the Synod or by the Synodical Council to provide supervision, educational or pastoral care to an Area. Such a Bishop may be a Suffragan Bishop or Assistant Bishop of a Diocese of the Synod or a retired Bishop of the Church. A Diocesan Bishop or Bishop Coadjutor may not serve as Area Bishop if his Diocese is already a member of the Synod.

ARTICLE VI

Section 1. A quorum of the legislative body of the Synod shall consist of a majority of the total number of active and Area Bishops entitled to sit, together with a majority of the total number of Deputies from the Dioceses or Areas entitled to representation.

Section 2. Unless otherwise provided, all elections and other votes shall be by a majority of the quorum present.

Section 3. In the absence of a quorum no business shall be transacted by the Synod except that the Synod may adjourn sine die or from day to day until a quorum is present.

ARTICLE VII

This Constitution shall become effective upon adoption by a majority vote in each of the Houses of the legislative body of the Synod present and voting. Amendments thereto shall be by two-thirds vote of those present in each of the two Houses.

ORDINANCES

I. Membership of the House of Deputies

Each Diocese or Area of the Synod shall have one Priest or Deacon and two members of the Laity as Deputies to the Legislative body of the Synod. The Clergy shall be canonically resident in the Diocese or within the Area they represent, and the Lay Deputies shall be communicants of this Church having canonical residence in the Diocese or within the Area they represent.

II. Synodical Council

Section 1. This Council shall consist of the elected officers and nine (9) members-at-large from among the Synod membership; one of these to be elected each year, for a three year term. The three shall not be from the same order. There shall be three Bishops, three Priests, and three members of the Laity, elected in rotating order.

Section 2. This Council shall meet at least annually at a time separate from the legislative body of the Synod and may meet further at the request of the President or at the request of any two members of the Council.

Section 3. The duties of this Council shall be:

a. To examine and respond to the needs expressed for program in the Synod.
b. To monitor income and expense budget and to reallocate as needed.
c. To receive the reports of the Task Forces and other bodies.
d. To measure and report on the fulfillment of the Synodical Statement of Purpose.
e. To be a Council of Advice for the President as needed.
f. To suggest policy statements for action of the legislative body of the Synod.
g. To recommend to the legislative body of Synod the Budget and Asking.
h. To create Task Forces as needed to carry out the purpose of the Synod and to terminate Task Forces when their existence no longer meets the purpose of the Synod.

III. Task Forces

Section 1. These shall be established by the Synodical Council or by action of the legislative body of the Synod.

Section 2. The President shall appoint a Convenor for each Task Force, who shall be the presiding officer of the Task Force.

Section 3. Members may be appointed by the President or by the Convenor with the approval of the President.

Section 4. Task Force expenditures shall be as approved by the legislative body of the Synod. Adjustments must be approved by the President and Treasurer. The Convenor of each Task Force shall submit an accounting of funds disbursed during the year within thirty (30) days after the end of each year.

IV. Budget

Section 1. The Synodical Council shall prepare the Budget and preseṅ it to the annual meeting of the legislative body of the Synod for approval.

Section 2. The financial support of the Synod is a voluntary responsibility of each member Diocese or Area. The President of the Synod shall cause to be submitted to the Synodical Council for transmission to the member Dioceses and Areas a request for a contribution. The amount of this request shall be sufficient, in addition to individual gifts and other sources of revenue, to fund the budget approved by the Synod.

V. Staff

The Synod may authorize the employment of an Executive Director or other staff as need exists and funds are available. Employment of staff shall be under such terms and conditions as the Synodical Council shall determine.

VI. Vote by Houses

In addition to other provisions for the House of Deputies and the House of Bishops to vote separately, except for election of officers, the two Houses shall vote separately whenever such a request is made by at least three Bishops or by deputations from a least two Areas or Dioceses.

Appendix 5.
Resolutions of the Synod, June 1–3, 1989

Resolution A. Episcopal Visitors

BE IT RESOLVED by the Episcopal Synod of America:

That we share with the Primates of the Anglican Communion the recognition that the proposal for Episcopal Visitors as adopted by the 1988 General Convention of The Episcopal Church has been criticized by both those in favor of and those against the ordination of women.

That we share with the Eames Commission Report that a plan of Episcopal Visitors "can be defended, as a necessary and strictly extraordinary anomaly in preference to schism."

That we recognize that the Constitution of The Episcopal Church in the provisions of Article II, Section 3, allows for the permission of Episcopal Visitors "in case of need," without regard to the Resolution of the Detroit General Convention.

That we believe bishops have a duty of being guardians of the Faith by virtue of the mission given by consecration and must obey God rather than men, especially if those men are bent on denying the admitted provisionality of women's ordinations and refusing to provide a pastoral alternative for those who do not accept such ordinations.

That we will respond to requests from congregations desiring the ministrations of bishops of this Synod, recognizing that any member of the clergy may be invited by the priest of a congregation to preach, baptize, celebrate the Eucharist, marry, bury the dead, hear confessions or anoint the sick, and give spiritual and pastoral guidance, as provided by Canon III. 14. 4 (a) (1).

That should such a request include the desire for the sacramental rite of Confirmation, a bishop of this Synod would first consult with the

Diocesan bishop of the congregation and seek permission as provided by Article II of the constitution and in the spirit of the Eames Commission Report.

That should such an approach be denied, the office of the Presiding Bishop would be sought as recommended by the Detroit General Convention.

That should this effort fail, the bishops of this Synod will nonetheless act in accordance with their mission given by consecration, obey God, and minister as requested. This Synod pledges its full support of its bishops in such a circumstance, and rejoices in their commitment to uphold and to continue the traditional apostolic ministry, including the preservation of the orthodox line of apostolic succession in the Episcopal Church.

Resolution B. On Use of the 1928 Book of Common Prayer

RESOLVED that diversities of liturgical custom are to be accepted provided the content of the Faith be kept whole:

That this Synod desires full tolerance for the conscientious use of the 1928 and 1979 versions of the Book of Common Prayer;

That this Synod expresses its deep concern over efforts to limit or eliminate the conscientious use of the previously authorized Book of Common Prayer;

That Christian charity shall rule in future discussions of the liturgical diversities which remain among us.

Resolution C. Actions by the Synodical Council

BE IT RESOLVED by the Episcopal Synod of America:

That the Synodical Council be authorized to speak for the Episcopal Synod of America in deliberations with the National Church or with other Provinces or bodies of the Anglican Communion.

That the Synodical Council shall be governed by policy statements duly adopted by the legislative body of the Synod.

That the Synod, wishing to proclaim the fullness of the Gospel and to affirm its desire for the unity of the Church, authorize its Council to speak and act on its behalf in deliberations with the Episcopal Church or with other Provinces or bodies of the Anglican Communion, and with the wider Church.

Resolution D. Ministering to All in the Church

BE IT RESOLVED by the Episcopal Synod of America:

That this Synod, its bishops, clergy and laity, will minister to all

Episcopalians and members of the Anglican Communion, of whatever views, within the Dioceses, Areas, congregations and institutions of the Synod. It is our express intent to be faithful to the truth as we have received it; nevertheless, we recognize that The Episcopal Church, the Anglican Communion as a whole, and our own Dioceses, Areas, congregations and institutions are divided on the issue of the ordination of women. To refuse to minister to those in our cures who cannot, in conscience, agree with us would be contrary to the will of Our Lord.

That in keeping with its obligation to maintain and propagate orthodox Anglicanism, which obligation has been acknowledged by the Archbishop of Canterbury, the Episcopal Synod of America will seek to provide priestly ministrations to those Episcopalians who for reasons of conscience are deprived of them.

That this Synod encourages lay people to identify one another in their localities and to support and develop Christian fellowship and assembly.

Resolution E. Resolution on Women's Ministries

BE IT RESOLVED by the Episcopal Synod of America:

That while recognizing that neither Scripture nor Catholic Tradition authorizes the ordination of women to the presbyterate or episcopate, we affirm the ministry of women in the life of the Church.

That we acknowledge that the Church has not always recognized and affirmed this ministry, nor provided adequate opportunities for women to exercise their ministry; and

BE IT FURTHER RESOLVED, That the legislative body of the Synod be instructed to consider the biblical and theological foundations for the exercise of ministries of women within the Church; the means and action to recognize, encourage, and celebrate these ministries; and to publish these findings, so as to make a positive statement of the direction of the Synod with regard to women's ministries.

Resolution F. Declaration of Communion

BE IT RESOLVED by the Episcopal Synod of America:

That as our Fathers declared in Chicago in 1886, we believe that all who have been duly baptized, with water in the name of the Father and of the Son and of the Holy Ghost, are members of the Holy Catholic Church.

That this basic baptismal unity in the Catholic Church remains in spite of our many divisions, joining all Christians in the one body of which Jesus Christ is the Head and all baptized persons are members.

That we therefore share a communion of *faith* with all who accept the supreme authority of Scripture and the truth of the Creeds; a communion of *moral principle* with all who defend the rights of the unborn and the sanctity of all human life, the sanctity of marriage as our Lord defined it, and with all who reject proposals to approve homosexual unions by liturgical services and blessings; a communion of *worship* with all who worship God according to His revelation of Himself, including all who worship according to the Book of Common Prayer, understood in a biblical and traditional way; a communion of the *ministry* of the word and sacraments with all who maintain the historic threefold ministry, recognizing that the episcopate and presbyterate are limited to males.

That while longing to be in communion with all Anglicans, and indeed all Christians, in all four ways, we are nevertheless thankful that we are in communion with some in the first three ways with whom we are not at present in communion in the fourth way also.

Resolution G. On Relations with Other Anglican Bodies in the USA

WHEREAS we are called to work for unity with all Christians according to the terms which are spelled out in the Chicago-Lambeth Quadrilateral;

AND WHEREAS there are particular jurisdictions and groups of the "continuing church" movement who have recently left the Episcopal Church or were disenfranchised for the same principles which have brought about the convening of this Synod;

AND WHEREAS the Reformed Episcopal Church has faithfully witnessed for over a century and has preserved the Anglican Evangelical tradition;

BE IT RESOLVED that this Synod applauds the courageous and faithful witness and leadership of these our fellow Christians, in the wider Anglican family; that this Synod covenants to pray for the ministry and mission of these bodies, recognizing their intention to uphold "the Anglican way of being Christian;" that this Synod establish relationships with these bodies, earnestly looking forward toward the day when full communion and, ultimately, union with them may be established.

Appendix 6.
Episcopal Synod of America Bishops

The Rt. Rev. Br. John-Charles
1474 Bushwick Avenue
Brooklyn, New York 11207
718-455-5963

The Rt. Rev. Stanley Atkins
1196 Saratoga Parkway
Oconomowoc, Wisconsin 53066
414-567-3695

The Rt. Rev. David S. Ball
62 South Swan Street
Albany, New York 12210
518-465-4737

The Rt. Rev. John B. Bentley
33 Old Mallory Road
Hampton, Virginia 23666
804-826-7134

The Rt. Rev. Charles F. Boynton
5 Bonito Drive
New Port Richey, Florida 34652
813-841-8222

The Rt. Rev. William H. Brady
47 South Reserve Avenue
Fond du Lac, Wisconsin 54935
414-921-0732

The Rt. Rev. A. Donald Davies
Suite 1112
6300 Ridglea Place
Fort Worth, Texas 76116
817-735-1675

The Rt. Rev. James L. Duncan
1020 Cotorro Avenue
Coral Gables, Florida 33146
305-667-0372

The Rt. Rev. Charles T. Gaskell
5442 North Iroquois Avenue
Glendale, Wisconsin 53217
414-962-8579

The Rt. Rev. Hal R. Gross
8255 Fairway Drive
Wilsonville, Oregon 97070
503-694-5318

The Rt. Rev. Clarence R. Haden
16828 Mossy Oak Drive
Dallas, Texas 75248
214-931-9691

The Rt. Rev. Joseph M. Harte
6300 N. Central
Phoenix, Arizona 85012
602-279-5539

The Rt. Rev. Edward H. MacBurney
3601 North North Street
Peoria, Illinois 61604
309-688-8221

The Rt. Rev. Robert H. Mize
4159 E. Dakota Avenue
Fresno, California 93726
209-227-6727

The Rt. Rev. Donald J. Parsons
308 W. Edgevale Place
Peoria, Illinois 61604
309-685-0548

The Rt. Rev. Clarence C. Pope
6300 Ridglea Place, Suite 1100
Fort Worth, Texas 76116
817-738-9952

The Rt. Rev. Paul Reeves
Route 4, Box 320
Hendersonville, North Carolina
28739
704-692-2792

The Rt. Rev. Victor H. Rivera
1919 Country Club Lane, South
Fresno, California 93727
209-251-9343

The Rt. Rev. David Schofield
4159 E. Dakota Avenue
Fresno, California 93726
209-227-6727

The Rt. Rev. W.C.R. Sheridan
16564 W. 18th B Road
Culver, Indiana 46511
219-842-2336

The Rt. Rev. William Stevens
Box 149
Fond du Lac, Wisconsin 54935
414-921-8866

The Rt. Rev. William C. Wantland
510 South Farwell Street
Eau Claire, Wisconsin 54701
715-835-3331

Appendix 7.
Overseas Bishops Attending the Synod, June 1–3, 1989

The Rt. Rev. George M. Sessford
Diocese of Moray, Ross and
 Caithness
Spynie House
96 Fairfield Road
Inverness IV3 5LL
UNITED KINGDOM

The Rt. Rev. Frederick C. Darwent
Diocese of Aberdeen and Orkney
16 Crown Terrace
Aberdeen AB1 2Hd
UNITED KINGDOM

The Rt. Rev. Paul Richardson
Anglican Church of Papua New
 Guinea
P.O. Box 893
Mount Hagen W.H.P.
PAPUA NEW GUINEA

The Rt. Rev. Philip E. Elder
Diocese of Windward Islands
Bishop's House
P.O. Box 128
St. Vincent, WEST INDIES

The Rt. Rev. John Hazlewood
Diocese of Ballarat
454 Wendouree Parade
Ballarat 3350
AUSTRALIA

The Rt. Rev. and Rt. Hon. Graham
 Leonard
Bishop of London
London House
8 Barton Street
London SWIP 3NE
ENGLAND

The Rt. Rev. Gerard Mpango
Diocese of Western Tanganyika
P.O. Box 13
Kasulu
Tanzania EAST AFRICA

The Rt. Rev. Harry S. Tevi
Diocese of Vanuatu
P.O. Box 238
Luganville, Santo
VANUATU, MELANESIA

Appendix 8.
Episcopal Synod of America Deputies

At the Synod, the first Synod legislature was elected to represent the six dioceses represented at the Synod by their bishop (Albany, Eau Claire, Fond du Lac, Fort Worth, Quincy, and San Joaquin) and from six "areas." Area I comprised the northeast, area II the southeast, area III the northern mid-west, area IV the southern midwest and part of the south, area V the northern plains states and the Pacific northwest, and area VI the southwest. Each diocese and each area elected one clerical and two lay deputies.

At the first meeting of the legislature, in November 1989, a wider representation was created. The deputies elected at the Synod were to serve at the second legislative meeting, in April 1990, after which the new deputies would be elected.

Mr. Bob Beadel
Rt. 3, Box 178A
Brownwood, Texas 76801
915-646-5104   *FORT WORTH

The Rev. Richard A. Cantrell
1000 S. Main Street
Moultrie, Georgia 31768
912-985-3676   *AREA II

Mr. Frederic C. Carlson
9 Windsor Drive
Clifton Park, New York 12065
518-371-7689   *ALBANY

Mr. David B. Chase
917 East "E" Street
Brunswick, Maryland 21716
301-834-7086   *AREA II

The Rev. Garrett M. Clanton
St. John's Episcopal Church
701 Hampshire
Quincy, Illinois 62301
217-222-3241   *QUINCY

The Rev. Robert D. A. Creech
W. 1823 Dean Avenue
Spokane, Washington 99201
509-328-1463   *AREA V

Mr. Richard R. Daly
725 S. Ridge Road
Green Bay, Wisconsin 54304
414-498-0955   *FOND DU LAC

Mr. Joe Dietrich
3619 Fourteen Mile Drive
Stockton, California 95209
209-957-3511   *SAN JOAQUIN

Mr. Robert V. Fairman
11809 First Street
Milan, Illinois 61264
309-787-1095   *QUINCY

Mr. William H. Flowers
P.O. Box 1338
Thomasville, Georgia 31799
912-226-9110   *AREA II

Mr. Robert Fluent
17 Windy Hill Road
Quincy, Illinois 62301
217-224-5194   *QUINCY

Mrs. Cris Fouse
25 Knoll Road, Rt. 2
Lewisville, Texas 75067
817-455-2397   *AREA IV

The Rev. Allan R. G. Hawkins
2212 Crooked Oak Court
Arlington, Texas 76012
817-277-4041   *FORT WORTH

Mrs. Catherine A. Heers
1752 Bishop Drive
Concord, California 94521
415-827-2661   *AREA VI

Mr. Gordon M. Kamai
298 Larkspur Plaza Drive
Larkspur, California 94939
415-924-9304   *AREA VI

Mr. David K. Leak
5093 Timberway Trail
Clarkston, Michigan 48016
313-625-4411   *AREA III

The Rev. J. Robert Maceo
848 Harter Road
Dallas, Texas 75218
214-321-6451   *AREA IV

Mr. William C. Mann
W. 1003 15th Avenue
Spokane, Washington 99203
509-747-6209   *AREA V

Mr. David P. Mills
26 Riverview Drive
Leetsdale, Pennsylvania 15056
412-741-8843   *AREA I

Mrs. Rita Moyer
503 Franklin Street
Ogdensburg, New York 13669
315-393-2334   *ALBANY

Mrs. Eunice Muenzberg
3625 Halsey Street
Eau Claire, Wisconsin 54701
715-832-8247   *EAU CLAIRE

The Rev. Edwin A. Norris
1133 N. LaSalle Street
Chicago, Illinois 60610
312-664-1271   *AREA III

The Rev. J. F. Titus Oates
240 Ashmont Street
Boston, Massachusetts 02124
617-436-6370   *AREA I

Mrs. Jo Ann Patton
3309 Marquette Court
Fort Worth, Texas 76109
817-924-5158   *FORT WORTH

Mr. Richard W. Phillips
1929 Valley Oaks Court
Irving, Texas 75061
214-254-2724   *AREA IV

Dr. Thomas C. Reeves
5039 Cynthia Lane
Racine, Wisconsin 53406
414-633-0509   *FOND DU LAC

Mrs. Shirley J. Rollinson
6514 N. Forrestal
Clovis, California 93612
209-298-8951   *SAN JOAQUIN

Mrs. Karen Sadock
67 West Shore Road
Dumont, New Jersey 07628
201-387-0240   *AREA I

The Ven. Donald A. Seeks
4159 E. Dakota Avenue
Fresno, California 93726
209-227-6727   *SAN JOAQUIN

Miss Elizabeth A. Servatius
98 East Lawrence Avenue
Springfield, Illinois 62704
217-789-7596   *AREA III

The Rev. Andrew L. Sloane
Grace Episcopal Church
630 Ontario Avenue
Sheboygan, Wisconsin 53081
414-452-9659   *FOND DU LAC

The Rev. Robert H. Tiling
Rt. 1, Box 234
Owen, Wisconsin 54460
715-229-2830   *EAU CLAIRE

Mr. Joseph Louis Vacca
3210 N. 97th Street, Apt. 179
Omaha, Nebraska 68134
402-571-5180   *AREA V

The Rev. Marshall J. Vang
23 Front Street
Schenectady, New York 12305
518-374-3163   *ALBANY

The Rev. Ralph T. Walker
1400 S. University Boulevard
Denver, Colorado 80210
303-777-5181   *AREA VI

Mrs. Janet E. Wantland
145 Marston Avenue
Eau Claire, Wisconsin 54701
715-832-2183   *EAU CLAIRE

Appendix 9.
English Support for ECM Synod

Almost 25 percent (138) of the membership of the General Synod of the Church of England sent a message of good wishes to those members of the Evangelical and Catholic Mission (ECM) of ECUSA, who met in special Synod at Fort Worth on June 1–3, 1989.

They included representatives from forty-one of the forty-four dioceses of the Church of England. Among them were the following:

Nine members of the House of Bishops
Both the prolocutors
Two deans and provosts
Eight archdeacons
Seven canons residentiary of cathedrals
Twenty-three other canons
Three Members of Parliament
Nine members of the Standing Committee of the General Synod
A further nineteen bishops and deans also indicated similar support.

The message read as follows:

TO THE CONVENING BISHOPS
OF THE ECM SPECIAL SYNOD

We welcome the initiative taken by the ECM to convene a Special Synod of Bishops, Clergy and Laity of ECUSA.

We share your concern at the continual erosion of the authority of Scripture and of the doctrinal and moral standards which are founded on it.

We recognize that current developments in ECUSA necessitate the provision of alternative orthodox episcopal oversight and appreciate the careful efforts you are making to this end.

We assure you of our prayers and support both during your current synod and in the future.

The Bishop of Blackburn, The Rt. Rev. Alan Chesters
The Bishop of Chichester, The Rt. Rev. Dr. Eric Kemp
The Bishop of Gibraltar in Europe, The Rt. Rev. John Satterthwaite
The Bishop of Leicester, The Rt. Rev. Dr. Richard Rutt, C.B.E.
The Bishop of London, The Rt. Hon. and Rt. Rev. Dr. Graham Leonard
The Bishop of Portsmouth, The Rt. Rev. Timothy Bavin
The Bishop Elect of Sodor and Man, The Venerable Noel Jones, C.B.
The Bishop of Truro, The Rt. Rev. Peter Mumford
The Bishop Suffragan of Edmonton, The Rt. Rev. Brian Masters
The Rev. Osmond Aisbitt
The Rev. Canon Derek Allen
The Rev. Canon Dennis Askew
The Ven. George Austin, Archdeacon of York
The Rev. Canon Michael Banks, Canon Chancellor of Leicester Cathedral
The Rev. John Barnes
The Rev. Dr. John Bishop
The Rev. John Boardman
The Rev. Canon Anthony Boult
The Rev. Canon Peter Boulton, Canon Residentiary of Southwell Minster, Prolocutor of the Lower House of the Convocation of York
The Rev. Christopher Boyle
The Rev. Canon Brian Brindley
The Rev. John Broadhurst
The Rev. Canon Donald Carter
The Rev. Canon Owen Conway
The Rev. Canon Chad Coussmaker
The Rev. Mark Ellis
The Very Rev. Richard Eyre, Dean of Exeter Cathedral
The Ven. Bernard Fernyhough, Archdeacon of Oakham, Canon Residentiary of Peterborough Cathedral
The Rev. Roger Fookes, V.R.D.
The Ven. John Galsford, Archdeacon of Macclesfield
The Rev. Peter Geldard
The Rev. Canon Derek Gibbs
The Rev. Canon Granville Gibson
The Rev. Richard Gillings
The Rev. Prebendary Dennis Goodman
The Rev. William Gornall
The Rev. Canon Roger Greenacre, Canon Chancellor of Chicester Cathedral

The Rev. Canon Terence Grigg
The Rev. John Hall
The Ven. Michael Henley, Q.H.C., Chaplain of the Fleet
The Rev. David Herbert
The Ven. Keith Hobbs, Archdeacon of Chichester
The Rev. Prebendary Graham Holley
The Very Rev. Laurence Jackson, Provost of Blackburn Cathedral
The Rev. Canon Barry Keeton
The Rev. Terence Knight
The Rev. David Lickess
The Rev. Prebendary Bernard Maddox
The Rev. Canon Thomas Mander
The Rev. Hugh Moore
The Rev. Prebendary Dr. Kenneth Noakes
The Rev. Fr. Richard Oaldey, C.R.
The Rev. Allan Park
The Rev. Prebendary John Pearce
The Rev. Canon Peter Peterken
The Rev. Professor Canon Roy Porter
The Rev. Reginald Priestnall
The Rev. Stuart Ramsden
The Rev. Michael Rear
The Ven. John Richards, Archdeacon of Exeter, Canon Residentiary of Exeter Cathedral
The Rev. Canon Raymond Ross
The Rev. Richard Rowe
The Rev. James Rushton
The Rev. Canon Gordon Sealy
The Rev. Canon John Short
The Ven. David Silk, Archdeacon of Leicester, Prolocutor of the Lower House of the Convocation of Canterbury
The Rev. Canon Peter Strange, Canon Residentiary of Newcastle Cathedral
The Ven. Ernest Stroud, Archdeacon of Colchester
The Rev. John Sykes
The Rev. Brian Tubbs
The Rev. Canon Leonard Tyzack
The Rev. Canon Michael Wilson, Canon Treasurer of Leicester Cathedral
The Rev. Stuart Wilson
The Rev. Humphrey York

The Rt. Hon. Michael Alison, M.P., Second Church Estates Commissioner
Mrs. May Ashworth, J.P.
Mr. Tom Booth
Mrs. Margaret Brown
Mrs. Patricia Brown
Mr. Peter Bruinvels
Dr. Terry Buckingham
Mrs. Mary Calvert
Mr. Maurice Chandler, C.B.E.
Mrs. Dorothy Chatterley
Mr. Oswald Clark, C.B.E.
Mr. Eric Cleaver
Mr. James Cheeseman
Mr. Nicholas Corbin
Mr. Michael Coombs
Mrs. Muriel Dawson
Mr. Peter Dixon
Mr. Nigel Edwards
Mr. Peter Ellis
Dr. Peter English
Mr. Andrew Fisher
Mr. Jeremy Fitzgerald-Thompson
The Hon. Jill Ganzoni, D.L.
Miss Wendy Geen
Mr. Philip Gore
Miss Clare Gough
The Rt. Hon. John Selwyn Gummer, M.P.
Mrs. Katherine Heidt
Dr. Margaret Hewitt
Dr. Mary Hobbs
Dr. Oliver Wright Holmes
Mr. Rowland Hopkins
Mr. Michael Hughes
Mrs. Alison Humphreys
Miss Patricia Hunsley
Mrs. Elizabeth Hunter
Mrs. Joanna Ingram
Mrs. Shirley Jackson
Mrs. Maryon Jagers
Mr. Andrew Knight
Mrs. Margaret Laird, Third Church Estates Commissioner

Mr. Julian Litten
Mrs. Patricia Mander
Mr. Vijay Menon
Mr. David Mills
Mrs. Allan Mills
Mrs. Florence Nobes
Mr. Marcel Noel
Mr. John Peckham
Mr. Russell Pond
Mr. Kenneth Rider
Mr. Adrian Scott
Mrs. Ruth Scrivener
Mrs. June Smalley
Mrs. Christine Smeaton
Miss Betty Smith, O.B.E.
Mr. Trevor Stevenson
Sir John Stokes, M.P.
Mr. Arthur Walsh
Mrs. Hilda Walter
Dr. Margaret White
Mrs. Norah Wilkinson
Mr. Frank Williams
Mr. Geoffrey Wippell

A similar message of support was received from the following:
The Rt. Rev. Peter Ball, C.G.A., Suffragan Bishop of Lewes
The Rt. Rev. Ronald Brown, Suffragan Bishop of Birkenhead
The Rt. Rev. Paul Borrough (formerly Bishop of Mashonaland and Assistant Bishop of Peterborough)
The Rt. Rev. Edmund Capper, O.B.E., Auxiliary Bishop in Europe (formerly Bishop of St. Helena)
The Rt. Rev. David Galliford, Suffragan Bishop of Bolton
The Rt. Rev. Anselm Genders, C.R. (formerly Bishop of Bermuda)
The Rt. Rev. George Giggall, O.B.E. (formerly Bishop of St. Helena and Assistant Bishop in Europe)
The Rt. Rev. John Hughes, Suffragan Bishop of Kensington
The Rt. Rev. John Klyberg, Suffragan Bishop of Fulham
The Rt. Rev. Edward Knapp-Fisher, Assistant Bishop of Chichester (formerly Bishop of Pretoria and Assistant Bishop of London and Southwark)
The Rt. Rev. Christopher Luxmoore, Archdeacon of Lewes and Hastings (formerly Bishop of Bermuda)

The Rt. Rev. John Maund, C.B.E., M.C. (formerly Bishop of Lesotho and Assistant Bishop of Worcester)
The Rt. Rev. Conrad Meyer (formerly Suffragan Bishop of Dorchester)
The Rt. Rev. John Mort, C.B.E. Assistant Bishop of Leicester (formerly Bishop of Northern Nigeria)
The Rt. Rev. Kenneth Newing, O.S.B. (formerly Suffragan Bishop of Plymouth)
The Rt. Rev. Vernon Nicholls, Assistant Bishop of Coventry (formerly Bishop of Sodor and Man)
The Rt. Rev. Anthony Tremlett (formerly Suffragan Bishop of Dover and Assistant Bishop of Gloucester)
The Very Rev. Eric Evans, Dean of St. Paul's, London
The Very Rev. Peter Moore, Dean of St. Alban's
The Rev. Roger Beckwith, Joint Secretary of the Association for the Apostolic Ministry
Mr. Arthur Leggett, Joint Secretary of the Association for the Apostolic Ministry